T5-BYG-432

THE CRAFT OF LETTERS IN ENGLAND

THE CRAFT OF
LETTERS
IN ENGLAND

A
Symposium
edited by
John Lehmann

LONDON: THE CRESSET PRESS 1956

820.904
R528c

100676

GEORGE PEABODY COLLEGE
LIBRARY
NASHVILLE, TENN.
GENERAL

First published in July 1956
by the Cresset Press Ltd., 11 Fitzroy Square, London, W.1
Printed in Great Britain by Western Printing Services Ltd.
Bristol

BELMONT COLLEGE LIBRARY

PR
473
.L38
1956

192214

Contents

8-8-57

Contents

The Craft of Letters
in England

Introduction

—

JOHN LEHMANN

I<small>T IS JUST</small> on a quarter of a century since the publication of a notable collection of essays by various hands, under the name of *Scrutinies*. In those two volumes, the contemporary state of literature (and the arts) in England was examined partly under general heads, but also partly in the persons of the remarkable authors, such as James Joyce, Virginia Woolf and T. S. Eliot, who were leaders in the revolutionary changes then taking place.

The present symposium has been devised to have a larger element of historical survey—of the years, roughly, since *Scrutinies* was published, though the accent falls on the post-war scene. Nor was any contributor asked to devote his specialist study to one author alone. For one thing, it would have been impossible in a book of limited length to cover the field with anything approaching adequacy if such individual studies had formed part of it. For another, the past three decades have seen the gradual disappearance of most of the literary giants, and their work has already been assessed from many critical points of view, and in detail. No English author who is alive today, with the exception of that unique survivor from the age of the giants, Mr. Eliot, can, I believe, claim the same formative power in contemporary literary activity.

B
1

It has been part of editorial policy to allow, in the inevitable overlap between some of the essays, differing judgements to appear in a free play of opinion. Nevertheless, certain interesting points of general, or almost general agreement emerge, either explicitly or implicitly. That we are living in an age without giants is one of them, that the outstanding figures of 1956 in creative literature have not the same stature as their predecessors of 1926; though, as Mr. Francis Wyndham hints in his essay, a few more years may completely change that comparison. Another point of agreement, which is particularly emphasized by Mr. Philip Toynbee and Mr. Roy Fuller, is that we have reached a historical moment when it is impossible not to write about the human condition in our time; that all serious writers now are deeply concerned about problems of belief, though Mr. Toynbee draws an important distinction between 'concern' and 'engagement' in the sense in which the latter word is understood on the continent of Europe. The fact that in our age most artists, unable entirely to accept the world-views of dogmatic Marxism on the one hand or dogmatic Christianity on the other, are obliged to adumbrate their own systems of values, makes the problem of belief, as Mr. Paul Bloomfield insists, the central problem of modern criticism; and is largely responsible, in Mr. Alan Pryce-Jones's view, for that great increase in recent years in the writing of, and evident appetite on the part of the public for personal stories—autobiographies, travel books and narratives of outstanding individual endeavour. It is a curious feature of this situation, which emerges from Mr. Maurice Cranston's study of *The Literature of Ideas*, that those who are designated as philosophers in England seem for the most

2

part to have hidden from it, devoting their energies largely to subtle (and often sadly arid) problems of semantics; though Mr. Cranston suggests that the pendulum is now at last beginning to swing the other way. As one sees from Miss C. V. Wedgwood's essay, it is among the historians that the great builders of systems have to be looked for in our age.

Miss Wedgwood makes the interesting point that the battle, in this country at least, between those who believe that history is a branch of literature and those who see the historian as primarily a sifter and organizer of the vast mass of raw material that has become available is really over; literature has won, and the contemporary battle is rather between the scholars and the popularizers. Mr. Stewart's study of biography during the period makes much of the same point: since Lytton Strachey the problem of the serious biographer has been to combine readability and the literary graces with sound research. The new channels of popularization are in fact one of the revolutionary features of mid-century, affecting more than the writing of history, biography and science. The great popular series of the Penguins and Pelicans, fathered by faith and canny foresight and advanced to their present level of importance by an unique combination of serious respect for what is good and a shrewd grasp of the problems of salesmanship, have brought, as Mr. Erik de Mauny points out, the major classics of foreign literature, ancient and modern, to a new readership of millions in the English-speaking world, and in translations that are essentially contemporary in style and language. Nothing is more remarkable than the determination of the Englishman during the last fifteen years not to deserve his traditional description of insular.

3

These cheap-priced series of books have not been the only agents of popularization. There have also been broadcasting—of crucial importance, as Mr. George Fraser indicates, in the livelihood of the contemporary poet—the 'reprint' book societies with their membership often of hundreds of thousands, the films which woo the successful author with fantastic extensions of fame and wealth, and the popular press. The influence of the last two cannot be said to have been entirely fortunate: they have both operated to widen the gap, long a feature of the American scene, between the best-seller and its less fortunate brethren among good books. A reading of Mr. L. D. Lerner's study of *The New Criticism* only emphasizes the inevitable conclusion: in the English literary world, the *middle-class* is now under increasing pressure from two sides, from those whose livelihood is bound up with the academic aspect of literature on the one side, and those who are occupied with the exploitation of all that can appeal in literature to a mass, and mainly non-intellectual audience. By middle class in this context I mean, not an income-bracket or standard of upbringing, but that body of intelligent readers who care for literature seriously as part of life, who can see through the specious appeal of four best-sellers out of five, whose opinions on the merits of a book are not swayed by irrelevant 'social' considerations and are equally uninfluenced by the pretensions of an academic high-priesthood who have a vested interest in the esoteric and difficult. Their voices seem to carry less far than they used to; they are the basis of a healthy literature; it will be a lamentable and ominous day if their position is finally over-run.

The occasion for the appearance of this symposium is the International Congress of the P.E.N., taking place in London for the first time for fifteen years. *The Craft of Letters in England* is a specific title: Scotland, Eire and Northern Ireland all have flourishing P.E.N. centres of their own, and have acted as hosts to the international society in recent years, and though it has obviously been impossible to keep the consideration of such key-figures as W. B. Yeats out of these essays—the attempt would have been absurd as well as undesirable—it seems necessary to point out that certain developments, as for instance the rise of a new school of consciously Scottish poets, have not been within the scope of this book. The occasion is one on which English writers, looking back on their achievements during the last twenty-five years, can, I believe, congratulate themselves on an abundance and vitality of literary achievement second to no other country. Only in the theatre, as Mr. T. C. Worsley so acutely reveals in his essay, has creative activity seemed to flag; but even there (as he hints) the phenomenon may prove to be transient, and has in any case coincided with a tremendous development in interpretation, especially of Shakespeare and the lesser great classics of our stage.

Biography

J. I. M. STEWART

LYTTON STRACHEY PUBLISHED his most famous biographical work, *Eminent Victorians*, as far back as 1918. But his influence has been so considerable that it will be useful to begin with some examination of his achievement. He revolutionized, Mr. E. M. Forster has said, the art of biography; and it is at least true that he made it vastly more entertaining. Whether the entertainment was altogether legitimate is an issue not quite easy to determine.

According to Strachey's friend Virginia Woolf it is the first duty of a biographer 'to plod, without looking right or left, in the indelible footsteps of truth'. Strachey seems to have subscribed to this. In the preface to *Eminent Victorians* he expresses the hope 'that the following pages may prove to be of interest from the strictly biographical no less than from the historical point of view', and claims that he has desired to 'elucidate certain fragments of the truth . . . to lay bare the facts of the case'. He says something, indeed, of the 'simple motives of convenience and of art'—but it is clear that the art invoked is such as an historian and biographer may properly use. The preface also tells us that the very abundance of the material available makes it impossible to write a formal history of

6

the Victorian Age. 'The direct method of a scrupulous narration' is hopeless, and the historian is recommended, therefore, to 'fall upon the flank, or the rear.' Strachey would presumably have denied that this martial metaphor removes us some way from elucidating truth and laying facts bare. Ignorance and misconception are the enemies that call forth generalship in the authentic historian or biographer. History that works round to the flank or the rear is by no means the same thing as backstairs history. It may expose ignobility; it is not itself ignoble. 'Je n'impose rien; je ne propose rien; j'expose.' Strachey in the last sentence of the preface makes this his own claim. But it is undeniable that much of his writing can be thus described only if the notion of exposure is given its full English colouring. Consider the essay on Arnold of Rugby:

> Henceforward the old rough-and-tumble, which was typified by the regime of Keate at Eton, became impossible. After Dr. Arnold, no public school could venture to ignore the virtues of respectability.

This from the closing paragraph has some appearance of being mildly edifying—as older biographies commonly considered it their duty to be. Anyone unacquainted with the drift of the English language in the period following *The Way of All Flesh* would be quite unaware of the faint derogatory implication of 'virtues of respectability'. In fact, Strachey has been presenting Thomas Arnold largely as a figure of fun. If Arnold is not wholly this, it is partly, indeed, because he possesses some estimable qualities, but rather more because he is muddled, stupid, vigorous and (in consequence) a minor danger to civilization. Strachey's most effective device is perhaps the embodying within a narrative of unflawed gravity of such *ipsissima verba* of his victim as some subsequent change of taste or conviction or intellectual climate disposes us to judge ridiculous. It is often, that is to say, chiefly the idiom of the Victorians that we are invited to find amusing.

Strachey has another resource in the deft bringing into focus of incongruities and disparities of which he affects to be unaware. Thus we read of Arnold:

> He was alarmed by the "want of Christian principle in the literature of the day", looking forward anxiously to "the approach of a greater struggle between good and evil than the world has yet seen"; and, after a serious conversation with Dr. Whately, began to conceive the necessity of considerable alterations in the Church Establishment.

The main device here is anti-climax; but it is supported by others. 'Serious', for instance, is so used as to point the hopeless absurdity inherent in the human situation; the more gravely Arnold and Whately wag their whiskers, the richer their corner of the cosmic comedy becomes. A further device is that of asserting some norm of rational feeling and behaviour, and setting beside this the actual persuasions and activities of the subject. Here is how Arnold is represented as facing the task of reforming Rugby:

> But how was he to achieve his end? Was he to improve the character of his pupils by gradually spreading round them an atmosphere of cultivation and intelligence? By bringing them into close and friendly contact with civilized men, and even, perhaps, with civilized women? By introducing into the life of his school all that he could of the humane, enlightened, and progressive elements in the life of the com-

munity? On the whole, he thought not. Such considerations left him cold, and he preferred to be guided by the general laws of Providence.

The tone of this prepares us for a crescendo of absurdities. It only remained, we are told, to discover what those general laws were; Arnold consulted the Old Testament; what was there revealed to him was the prefectorial system. And so eventually:

> the younger children, scourged both by Dr. Arnold and by the elder children, were given every opportunity of acquiring the simplicity, sobriety, and humbleness of mind, which are the best ornaments of youth.

Here, it is suggested, was the keystone of Arnold's system. But the privileged small boys had required of them other forms of receptiveness as well. When the headmaster preached:

> the whole character of the man—so we are assured—stood at last revealed. His congregation sat in fixed attention . . . while he propounded the general principles both of his own conduct and that of the Almighty, or indicated the bearing of the incidents of Jewish history in the sixth century B.C. upon the conduct of English schoolboys in 1830.

It is odd to reflect that one of Strachey's masters in all this is Thomas Arnold's son. When Dr. Arnold, puzzled by all the mysteries of Faith, is further disquieted by learning that 'Unitarianism is becoming very prevalent in Boston', and yet more deeply perplexed by his observation that 'in Chronicles xi. 20, and xii. 2, there is a decided difference in the parentage of Abijah's mother', we might be listening to the voice of Matt, exposing the disproportions and absurdities into which we may be

9

betrayed when we lose contact with the divine moderation of the spirit of Greece. Or again when we are told of the father that he 'had become convinced of the duty of sympathizing with the lower orders ever since he had made a serious study of the Epistle of St. James', the deliciously muted quality of the satire is thoroughly reminiscent of the son.

But as a writer Strachey possesses one power denied alike to Matthew Arnold and to most of his own imitators. Like two or three of the greatest ironists—Swift, Gibbon, Voltaire—he has a superb narrative gift. Strachey is a story-teller—and what we have to dwell on, of course, is the ambiguity lurking in the term. Since few lives are so much of a piece as not to command at least some ebb and flow of sympathy, it is to be questioned whether artistic effects depending upon an unflawed texture of irony are apposite in biography. But it is yet more questionable whether the story should be made a better story by fudging the facts. Of the essay on Cardinal Manning one is tempted to say that it reads like one of the great novels of the world. But it cannot honestly be described as 'plodding in the indelible footsteps of truth'. Again, the portrait of General Gordon is undeniably a masterpiece; but its famous brandy-bottle turns out to be of the most questionable provenance. Once we are made aware of this, we must read in perpetual suspicion. Take one tiny touch about Arnold:

His legs, perhaps, were shorter than they should have been.

What devilry, we suddenly wonder, lurks in that 'perhaps'? The answer, it seems, is a great deal.

Is this irresponsibility to be defended in an enquirer into and interpreter of historical personages? There seem to be two views on the matter. 'Even when they are wrong they seem alive', says Mr. Forster, rejoicing in Strachey's creations. Others find the irresponsibility monstrous. Bertrand Russell has told us that when he read *Eminent Victorians* in prison he laughed so loudly that a warder came round to his cell to remind him that he was in a place of punishment—but nevertheless his considered view of Strachey's achievement is severe:

> He was indifferent to historical truth and would always touch up the picture to make the lights and shades more glaring and the folly or wickedness of famous people more obvious. These are grave charges.

Following upon all this, various questions suggest themselves. Should a line be drawn between biography as light as Strachey's wit and biography as serious as Dr. Whately's conversation? What about a code of ethics for the historical novelist? If *Eminent Victorians* must be condemned as holding up a maliciously distorting mirror to its subjects, then what about Sir Max Beerbohm's cartoons? They certainly often serve 'to make the folly of famous people more obvious'. What about Bertrand Russell's own brilliant power to make earlier philosophers—Hegel, for example—supremely ridiculous? Or how many of the arts employed by Strachey in the Cardinal Manning are to be found in Russell's account of the Church's dealings with Galileo? Is it bad to be 'indifferent to historical truth' in the interest of malicious glee, like Strachey; but all right to be so in the interest of a sentimental morality, like Carlyle? And what purely literary equipment, anyway, may the historian or biographer safely be allowed?

A reflective reading of Strachey's work is delightful

in itself. It is also an excellent preliminary to any consideration of the canons of modern biography.

Whatever we may think of the ethics of Strachey's dealings with the eminent, we must admit that his books have proved highly acceptable. The writer established a manner, but he also met a taste. He was part of a broad movement towards the searching and the astringent; and as a predominant note this was something new in English biography. Mr. H. W. Garrod, a circumspect critic who has spoken of ours as the Golden Age of Vulgarity, has yet derided Bishop Christopher Wordsworth for supposing 'the grandeur of life to consist in its decorum, and the art of biography to be realized in edification'. Dr. Johnson, the greatest of the English biographers, would have been surprised at this levity in a Professor of Poetry at Oxford. Both decorum and edification were essentials in Johnson's canon, and he could seriously debate whether it was justifiable to reveal that Addison drank. (He decided that it was, since the exhibition of a flaw in the character of a man almost totally virtuous may prevent our being discouraged to an undesirable degree by the contemplation of our own more abundant weaknesses.) From Izaak Walton onwards the exemplary motive has always been strong. There have indeed been plenty of severe and even savage portraits—Clarendon's of the Earl of Arundel is a good example—but in the major writers (Boswell, Southey, Lockhart, Festing Jones) there is invariably an assumption that we are being afforded a gratifying vision of persons who on balance are overwhelmingly estimable. The crimes and follies of mankind are painfully evident to us all; but biography is not the right theatre for their exhibition at large. There, as in tragedy according to the conception of Aristotle, they should have no more prominent place than is necessary for the furtherance of other designs.

It is clear that in the later Victorian period these wholesome persuasions were relied upon to excess, so that some reaction became inevitable. The changed attitude is evident in what it came to be thought proper to write—or to permit being written—about relatives and friends. The Coleridges—a family variously eminent—were unable to conceal that the poet Samuel Taylor Coleridge had been somewhat lacking in the attributes of a prudent citizen; but they could at least discourage any disposition to make much of him, or to unearth the details of his career. Wordsworth's illegitimate daughter was for long a dark family secret, and a distinguished French scholar who had enjoyed the friendship of his descendants felt himself in honour bound to preserve this reticence when he himself came upon the truth. The materials for a life of Matthew Arnold descended to the generation succeeding his own only after drastic censorship and destruction. Under such conditions 'authorised' biographies were bound to be stuffy and flabby. Candour was not to the public taste. When in 1907 Edmund Gosse published *Father and Son*, a book which few now find shocking, the *Times Literary Supplement* began its review:

> The author of this book has no doubt settled it with his conscience how far in the interests of popular edification and amusement it is legitimate to expose the weaknesses and inconsistencies of a good man who is also one's father.

When with *Left Hand! Right Hand!* Sir Osbert Sitwell in 1944 embarked upon a somewhat similar enterprise on a larger scale there were no noticeable head-shakings of this sort. The making of elegant literary diversion out of one's immediate forebears, a practice long current among novelists, had become sanctioned for biographers. It is a kind of writing that invites disaster, but which can come off brilliantly when the tone is right. Sir Timothy Eden's *The Tribulations of a Baronet* (1933), an account of that Sir William Eden who fell foul of Whistler, is a small masterpiece here; and a more recent example is Mr. Anthony Glyn's *Eleanor Glyn* (1955). Viola Meynell's *Alice Meynell* (1929) and Sir Charles Tennyson's *Alfred Tennyson* (1949) are distinguished works of greater intrinsic importance in this category.

As with relatives, so with friends. That sort of volume of reminiscences in which a whole circle of acquaintance was touched in largely in terms of sentiment or panegyric fell out of fashion, and veracity and entertainment alike raised bolder heads. A book of this sort, if predominantly atrabilious in character, is seldom pleasing; but even malice will pass when it is at once gentle and well ballasted with humour and affection. Sir William Rothenstein's two volumes of *Men and Memories* (1931 and 1932) are examples of high success here, as are the *Portraits* (1931) and posthumously published *Memories* (1953) of Desmond MacCarthy. Three formal biographies based upon personal knowledge are the *George Moore* (1936) and *W. B. Yeats* (1942) of Joseph Hone, and Mr. Rupert Hart-Davis's *Hugh Walpole* (1952). The last-named has an assured claim to be among the half dozen best biographies of the century.

At an extreme of the new tendency, and of quite different effect, are those biographies in which the balance of sympathy is felt as tilted sharply away from the subject.

Here, in a sense, we are back with Strachey—who yet must be put on record as refraining from any public exercise of his talents upon those at whose table he had sat. Mr. Robert Gathorne-Hardy's *Recollections of Logan Pearsall Smith* (1949) is a good example of a memoir of considerable warmth and charm which yet fails to avoid some of the submerged hazards inherent in any intimate chronicle of the ebb and flow of a friendship. But what comes most immediately to mind at this point is the mass of biographical writing which has appeared on D. H. Lawrence.

Few modern writers can have had so many candid friends as Lawrence, and as we ourselves make the acquaintance of some of them we may come to feel how temerarious is the proposal to sort out, *coram populo*, one's relations with such a man. One of these books (1950) has a title-page that merits reproduction:

PORTRAIT OF A GENIUS, BUT . . .
(The Life of D. H. Lawrence, 1885–1930)
by
RICHARD ALDINGTON

"When a true Genius appears in the World, you may know him by this Sign, that the Dunces are all in Confederacy against him."   JONATHAN SWIFT.

In fact, the confederacy is one in which Mr. Aldington lands himself. His proposal has clearly been to hold the balance between an irresistible Lawrence and an impossible Lawrence, between a writer of profound originality and a writer of clap-trap. But as the book develops it takes on the character of an excavation. The biographer is progressively discovering how he really feels about his subject underneath; and as decorum is, by definition, ruled out, we finally get what is, indeed, the truth—but the truth about precisely this. Just half-way through, for example, we are pointed to an episode (in one of Lawrence's novels) which is 'instructive', and upon which Mr. Aldington comments:

> It shows that once his moods of malice or frenzied rage had evaporated Lawrence was quite prepared to forget and even forgive all the insults and upsets he inflicted on his friends. He bore his victims absolutely no ill-will—or at least not until he came to write about them.

As one reviewer remarked, the writer is at once inviting our pity for a crucified Lawrence and unable to resist an inclination to give the nails an extra knock on his own account. If one finds this ambivalence displeasing one may take comfort from the fact that there is no evidence of Mr. Aldington's bearing Lawrence any ill will—'at least not until he came to write about' him.

The trouble with such a book as this, we may say, lies in the impurity of the form, biography becoming too much a vehicle for self-expression. Related considerations apply to Mr. Middleton Murry's two books: *Son of Woman* (1931) and *Reminiscences of D. H. Lawrence* (1933). The degree of personal involvement, the urgency of rights and wrongs to be sorted and argued, is too great. Dr. Johnson declared that nobody can write the life of a man but those who have ate and drunk and lived in social intercourse with him. And, in his biography of Richard Savage, Johnson produced his own triumph of this sort. But perhaps it is fair to murmur that he never had to tackle Lawrence—and in the twentieth century. Certainly when Lawrence himself attempted, in his introduction to *Memoirs of the Foreign Legion* (1924), a

16

biographical sketch of Maurice Magnus, a character holding some affinity with Savage, he came very notably short of Johnson's large charity. And if the acrid emphasis is largely temperamental, it is in part a matter of a more general intellectual and moral climate. The most impressive biographical studies of Lawrence have been by persons standing in some independence from this: notably that published in 1935 by E. T. (the Miriam of *Sons and Lovers*); Frieda Lawrence's *Not I, but the Wind* (1934); and Harry T. Moore's *The Intelligent Heart* (1955). The last is a scholar's book, and belongs to a category of biographies yet to be considered.

Strachey, an admirer of Racine, was a penetrating psychologist. Some of his successors—notably Philip Guedalla in books like *Palmerston* (1926) and *The Queen and Mr. Gladstone* (1932)—were without much natural endowment in this particular, and got along by imitating his picturesque evocations and his surface wit. Others, attracted by the growing prestige of the writings of Freud and Jung, came to regard the requisite equipment as acquirable through a judicious frequentation of appropriate text-books. And indeed the novel and dynamic theories of the mind, together with the innumerable systematic investigations of human character and motive upon which they were based, seemed likely to have a large and legitimate influence upon the craft of biography. But not all the early essays were successful. Particularly unfortunate was the attempt to reinforce Strachey's deflationary technique by touching in the indignities and absurdities which a suitable reading of unconscious motivations and the like can lend to almost any act or attitude. The *Matthew Arnold* (1928) of Hugh

Kingsmill is a mild example of this unhappiness. But Freud was potent, too, with more serious writers. We have seen that in the previous generation Wordsworth's liaison with Annette Vallon remained within the category of disreputable secrets. By 1930, in Sir Herbert Read's *Wordsworth*, the incident is seen as determining the whole course of the poet's development, and the supporting argument is heavy with mechanisms which are essentially those postulated by psycho-analysis. The records of an actual life, however, no less than of a dream, prove perplexingly susceptible of widely differing interpretations even in terms of the same basic assumptions; and lately Mr. F. W. Bateson, in his *Wordsworth: A Reinterpretation* (1955), has set the emphasis not upon Wordsworth's mistress but upon his sister, with whom his relations are discovered to us as verging on the incestuous.

In general, then, it may be said that the depth-psychologies have been helpful to the biographer mainly when exploited with marked discretion, while at the same time they are far too significant to be ignored. Two recent works on Henry James enforce this. Mr. Leon Edel, in his *Henry James: The Untried Years* (1953), although he avoids positively laying the Master upon the analyst's couch, yet displays again and again a fascinating acuteness which only some study of analytic technique would make possible. Thus he notices how James, in a list of likely names for fiction set down when he was fifty, included *Ledward* and then improvised several variants: *Ledward-Bedward-Dedward-Deadward*. For the novelist, clearly, to be led to the marriage bed was to be dead, and 'Henry James accordingly chose the path of safety. He remained single.' When we turn to *Young Henry*

James (1955), and the writer, Mr. Robert C. Le Clair, tells us of his 'constant effort . . . to avoid psycho-analysis', which he equates with 'arbitrary inter-pretation, pet theories, and all the other glamorous but dangerous byways which often tempt the biographer beyond what he is able to bear', we are likely to feel that the ensuing book, even if abundantly meritorious, will prove rather an old-world affair. If biography is to be, above all, a record of personality, it cannot, we may repeat, neglect those branches of psychology which seek to trace in the inner development of individuals the working of intelligible laws. Yet how much of the bio-grapher's equipment must remain that which is, broadly speaking, traditional, is illustrated—and it could no-where be illustrated more significantly—in the two volumes which have so far appeared (1953 and 1955) of Dr. Ernest Jones's *Sigmund Freud: Life and Work.* If this is one of the best biographies of the age, it is partly because of the literary tact which the writer has dis-played in any deployment of the resources of psycho-analysis upon the figures of its founder and his disciples. The relationships of these men, isolated by the strange-ness of their science and (as regards the majority) by their race, and each almost professionally obliged to believe himself possessed of a radical insight into the motives and dispositions of the others, were manifestly extremely difficult. Dr. Jones expresses, but does not parade, his own technical insight into the group. But at the same time he builds up his picture of Freud himself with all the prescriptive resources of the orthodox bio-grapher.

While the serious application of Freud's ideas (as also, possibly, of Jung's) to the practice of biography is thus, at least potentially, of great importance, there may be discerned a tendency, facilitated by the desuetude of the old canons of reticence, to seek biographical material in subjects lending themselves to a popular, and more or less sensational, 'psychological' approach. Ruskin is an important Victorian writer, but one, it must be suspected, who is comparatively little read. He is, however, decidedly a 'case'—walking, somebody has said, a tight-rope between madness and misery. That what is pathological and harrowing has great fascination for the present age is evinced by the number of biographical studies that he has provoked. The most brilliant of these, Mr. Peter Quennell's *John Ruskin: Portrait of a Prophet* (1949), is genuinely perceptive. Yet Mr. Quennell's concentration upon what he calls 'the mystery of an individual character' results in some neglect of that to which, in any reasoned estimate, Ruskin must be judged to owe his fame. If we try to imagine Dr. Jones's book rewritten on Mr. Quennell's principles we may see in this sort of biography a disproportion of which the *reductio ad absurdum* is to be found in Monsieur André Maurois's *Ariel* (Paris, 1923), a biographical sketch of Shelley, delightfully executed, which omits any notice of his writing poetry. If we take the simple view that a man's creations are an essential part of himself, rather than (as is indeed tenable) something won from the void and in no essential relationship to his 'life', then we shall probably judge Ruskin less well served by Mr. Quennell, or by Derrick Leon in his *Ruskin: The Great Victorian* (1949), than by Dr. Joan Evans in her *Ruskin* (1954), a balanced account of the man and the quality of his achievement.

The establishment of the new psychology has had another effect. Recondite enquiry into concealed motives

and unconscious purposes is its principal stock-in-trade,
and it habituates us to the notion that the truth about a
man may long elude even the intent observation of
persons unprovided with some necessary clue or key to
his mystery. This disposition of things has favoured that
sort of interpretative biography which Mr. T. S. Eliot
makes fun of as:

> revealing for the first time the gospel of some dead sage,
> which no one has understood before; which owing to the
> backward and confused state of men's minds has lain un-
> known to this very moment.

'The desire to compose the life of an individual as
illustration of some extraneous theory or conception' is
a familiar enough phenomenon, and Sir Harold Nicolson
has listed it, along with the hagiographic impulse, as the
principal occasion of 'impure' biography. Mr. Middleton Murry's *Keats and Shakespeare* (1925), *Blake* (1933)
and *Shakespeare* (1936) are examples; and even his more
regularly biographical and almost wholly admirable
Swift (1954) admits something of the same ambiguity
of aim. These books are also apposite as reminding us how
indeterminate, within the general province of literature,
has become the boundary between biographical and
critical study. Johnson's formula in the *Lives of the Poets*
had for long almost universal acceptance, and seems to
have been imposed, for instance, upon the contributors
to the well-known 'English Men of Letters' series.
But this has largely broken down. Novels, plays, poems
and paintings are treated as so much documentary
material at the biographer's command; he uses them
much as the analyst uses dreams and free associations
and parapraxes. Correspondingly, what can be established

or supposed of the individual psychology of the artist is carried over to the analysis and evaluation of his work. Whether this confluence is judged advantageous to either criticism or biography will depend upon the view taken of the relationship—touched upon above—between a man and his creation. A significant divergence of view makes the substance of *The Personal Heresy* (1939), a lively controversy between Professor C. S. Lewis and Dr. E. M. W. Tillyard which every biographer would do well to study. On this large topic only one further observation is possible here. It does sometimes indubitably happen that a close study of the man going about his diurnal occasions has the effect of brilliantly illuminating the artist at his creative task. Mr. Robert Gittings's *The Living Year* (1954) does this for Keats, and is perhaps the most notable genetic study of a body of English poetry since John Livingston Lowes's *The Road to Xanadu.*

The achievement and influence of scholarship have alike been important. While it is true that indifferent scholars have produced almost as many stodgy biographies as purely popular writers have produced superficial or vulgar ones, good scholars have given us some of the best work of all. The following have been particularly notable: Lord David Cecil's biography of Cowper, *The Stricken Deer* (1929), and his subsequent *The Young Melbourne* (1939) and *Lord M.* (1955); Mr. Edmund Blunden's *Leigh Hunt* (1930); Mr. Hugh I'Anson Fausset's life of Wordsworth, *The Lost Leader* (1933); Professor J. M. Neale's *Queen Elizabeth* (1934); R. W. Chambers's *Sir Thomas More* (1935); Miss Veronica Wedgwood's *Strafford* (1935) and *William the Silent* (1944); Miss Janet Adam Smith's *Robert Louis Stevenson*

(1937); Sir George Trevelyan's *Grey of Falloden* (1937); Miss Catherine Maclean's life of Hazlitt, *Born Under Saturn* (1943); Miss Carola Oman's *Nelson* (1947) and *Sir John Moore* (1953); Professor Oswald Doughty's *A Victorian Romantic: Dante Gabriel Rossetti* (1949); Mr. and Mrs. Hanson's *The Four Brontës* (1949); Mr. James Pope-Hennessey's *Monckton Milnes* (1949); Mrs. Cecil Woodham-Smith's *Florence Nightingale* (1950), a book both of the highest merit in itself and interesting as enabling one to study the selective principles upon which Strachey worked; Mr. Noel Annan's *Leslie Stephen* (1951); and Mr. Roy Harrod's *John Maynard Keynes* (1951). It must be added that two of the most justly acclaimed historical biographies of the age are the work not of professional scholars but of statesmen: the massively conceived and vigorously executed *Marlborough* (1933–38) of his descendent, Sir Winston Churchill; and Mr. Duff Cooper's slighter and less Corinthian *Talleyrand* (1932). Among all these it is perhaps notable that only Mr. Harrod's book could be approximately classified as an 'official' biography. Even so, and although the subject commands the writer's whole-hearted affection and loyalty, it is an admirably objective book.

And here indeed we approach the best quality that contemporary biography can show. For it was rashly, after all, that Sir Harold Nicolson stigmatized as conducing to 'impure' biography 'the desire to celebrate the dead'; and that he laughed at Sir Sidney Lee's finding a mainspring of the kind in 'an instinctive desire to do honour to the memories of those who, by character and exploits, have distinguished themselves from the mass of their countrymen.' Lee is speaking of an impulse that is real and valid—and one that was acknowledged long before Tacitus wrote the opening sentence of his *Agricola*. If Lee himself produced his life of King Edward the Seventh at some rather different prompting, the fact is no doubt to be regretted, but it by no means invalidates the general proposition. And that even the official biography of a recently deceased monarch may bear it out is shown, by a happy irony, in a work which Sir Harold himself was to achieve just a quarter of a century after he had committed himself to the opinion quoted. *King George the Fifth: His Life and Reign* (1952) is a triumphant success—and precisely because 'the instinctive desire to do honour' is present, and rationally directed upon an adequate subject. The King was a person entirely undistinguished alike in intellect and imagination. It is not concealed from us that his mind remained in many regards as unformed as his handwriting; and that it came more easily to him to take note of a change of wind in the literal than in any metaphorical and political sense. Yet he possessed certain estimable—even noble—moral qualities which his office tested, tempered, and rendered valuable to his country. We are left with the feeling of having met someone worth knowing for his own sake—a man who, in a different walk of life, might have caught and held the respect and interest of, say, Joseph Conrad.

Finally it may be suggested that, although nothing is more detestable than fictionalized biography, the pure biographer may yet have learnt something from those great novelists in whom so much of the imaginative energy of Europe has concentrated itself during the past hundred years. Mr. J. G. Lockhart's *Cosmo Gordon Lang* (1949) is a thoroughly veridical biography, yet the kind of knowledge of the Archbishop to which it attains is curiously akin to the novelist's—and, as in a novel, keen perception generates sympathy for a personality not, perhaps, very immediately endearing. At least we may notice that some of the best biographies—and biographies notable for that emphasis upon positive sympathy which we have been commending—are themselves the work of distinguished novelists. There may be instanced John Buchan's *Montrose* (1928) and *Cromwell* (1934); Mr. E. M. Forster's *Goldsworthy Lowes Dickinson* (1934), Virginia Woolf's *Roger Fry* (1940); Mr. Aldous Huxley's biography of F. Leclerc du Tremblai, *Grey Eminence* (1941); Mr. Anthony Powell's *John Aubrey and his Friends* (1948); and Mr. H. E. Bates's *Edward Garnett* (1950).

The Personal Story

ALAN PRYCE-JONES

I T IS ONE of the most surprising facts of human history that people of all kinds should have succeeded for so long in concealing their passionate interest in themselves. They wrote letters, poems, stories about themselves, it may be; some, like Casanova, told significant lies round their private lives; like Rousseau, others tried to give their actions in retrospect a sense of direction. But very few, or none, obeyed the compulsion of an innumerable horde of modern writers to search every cranny of the mind for some detail of remembrance chosen to shore up the delicate fabric of a personality.

Of course we catch our glimpses. Out of the darkness of antiquity a figure emerges here and there. Horace in one way, St. Augustine in another, tell us something of their inner reality. A sharply etched line in the letters of Queen Elizabeth or a snap from Dr. Johnson do nearly as much, however. We can tell what kind of people we are reading about, but we are not allowed, even in overt confessions, to get very much closer. Their childhood, for instance—the staple diet of the modern autobiographer: we seldom hear anything about that except in the heightened tone of, for instance, a Wordsworth. The loving attention to a place or a period, the lost causes, the conversation of others, the eccentricity of friends, the conscious eclipse of innocence, the delights of betrayal— all of them themes which are permanently a part of human existence—seemed to our ancestors unworthy of notice. On the evidence, they had no undirected moments. They did not sing in their baths or talk to themselves in the street; they avoided mortification except out of virtue; they never got into a muddle and stayed there a lifetime. They might observe and record others doing such things but never themselves.

Experience, in fact, was to be used as a kind of compost: an uninteresting matter for study, but one which, if properly manipulated, could nourish a crop of splendid flowers. Clearly the plays of Shakespeare are exactly such flowers; clearly, too, Shakespeare preferred to use his experience after this objective fashion rather than to offer himself up as a human being. And it is fascinating to speculate on the reasons which led a whole generation of writers suddenly to abandon the objective use of their own experience in order to try and set down on paper not a construction prompted by life but as nearly as possible the appearances of life itself.

The moment seems to have come during the first world war. Perhaps that was the moment in time when mankind first became fully aware of its own fragility. All the props gave at once. The universal comforter, money, lost its only point. It ceased to be a defence against an unkind world. Religion was at a low ebb. For one unknown Péguy there were a score of prelates blessing the guns. Society itself, however beautifully stratified in appearance, turned out to be no more solid than a *millefeuille* when its organization was attacked. The one thing which remained constant in a shifting world was the human personality.

By a coincidence, furthermore, study of heart and mind had been worked into the forefront of modern science. We no longer merely believed ourselves to be fascinating; science assured us that we really were. We had a duty to take stock of ourselves, to tabulate our responses. And simultaneously everyone who could remember a past which, by contrast with the present, seemed paradisal, felt it a duty to save all that could be saved from the ruins of time.

That was the mood of a book like Maurice Baring's *The Puppet Show of Memory*. It is an unexpectedly impersonal book, in which the writer uses himself as a lens to focus the past. But not all the past, by any means. For instance, one chapter closes with a brief sentence to the effect that towards a given moment Baring was received into the Catholic Church. A writer today would hardly have shown himself so economical. We should have had each step in his *peripeteia* charted out for us, each doubt recorded, each triumph modestly set in the balance. But in the things which touched him most Baring was typical of an older generation. He evades the issues of faith and love and friendship in order to allow his readers as serene a gaze as possible upon chosen aspects of a happy past. Other writers of approximately the same age and kind did likewise. The memoirs of Edith Wharton, say, or Mrs. Humphry Ward are above all decorous. The truths of imagination meant more to such writers than the incongruous truths of daily life.

Younger writers, however, already felt differently. There is a sharp point, for instance, in the title of Mr. Robert Graves's *Good-bye to All That*. The past was not

28

always halcyon. Sometimes it had to be exorcised. Sometimes, too, it seemed too mysterious to be presented directly. That, no doubt, is why Mr. Siegfried Sassoon withheld his name from *The Memoirs of a Fox-hunting Man*. Primitive peoples and mystics know the danger in naming things, and it seems that for a time at least Mr. Sassoon shared their apprehensions.

The need to evoke or exorcise a happy past still persists, and it is interesting to see how very much braver writers have become in facing squarely their own beginnings. The glow of the years before 1914 is now more lurid than it used to be, but not less conspicuous. Would Lady Emily Lutyens, one wonders, have used the same tone of voice had she published *A Blessed Girl* thirty years ago? A book less like *The Puppet-Show of Memory* can hardly be imagined; and yet Lady Emily in childhood breathed much the same air as Maurice Baring. Can the difference be accounted for simply in terms of divergent personalities, or is it easier today to speak out than it was even in the emancipated 1920s?

It is certainly very much harder to shock a reader than it was twenty or thirty years ago—a fact which must partly account for the decline of the novel. When both violence and innuendo fail to startle, a writer has to fall back on his last weapon: the truth. And it looks as if even the ultimate veil—idealization of the truth—were being stripped away little by little. Mr. Graves is answerable for some of this. When it came out in 1929 his autobiography seemed both pungent and entrancing to those who, like myself, were young. We enjoyed the snorts of elder rage, the threats of libel, the atmosphere of recrimination in which the book eventually appeared, partly because we were young enough to enjoy a good row, but partly, too, because we were excited to emulation by the firmness with which Mr. Graves tackled his own dead self and the spirit with which he breathed life back into the bleached bones of the past.

I imagine that a similar spirit must have animated Mr. Cyril Connolly a few years later, when he published *Enemies of Promise*. That book is a key-book of its kind, for not only is it extremely entertaining in its account of a most untypical boyhood but it also makes a series of authoritative statements on one of the central problems of the modern writer: the difficulty of writing at all. It is thus a book which moves in a spiral. Writing brilliantly about not writing, Mr. Connolly gyrates round the mood which has prompted the best of modern autobiographical records. Our talents, our advantages, our happiness, our background, he suggests, all conspire to kill our promise. We are born at the wrong time; we are taught the wrong way; we rob ourselves, almost as ardently as we are robbed, of the possibilities within us. Mr. Connolly's is only an extreme case among those which have become typical of imaginative writers in this country. Either they go back in time to a period when (seen from a safe distance) life appears steady and coherent, or they jump forward to an imaginary future. The choice lies between *A House and Its Head* and *1984*. The present tense, however, is equally unacceptable to both parties, since the days flash by in a riot of dislocated images. Autobiography offers one solution to the writer; if he can explain nothing else he can perhaps explain himself.

There is something slightly suspect, however, about the reluctance with which our writers attack the present. It is odd, for instance, that in the United States, where the present appears much more lively than in England, memorable autobiographies are generally produced either by public figures writing for the record or by men whose experience of life has been idiosyncratic enough to deserve a memorial—men like Mr. Alfred Kazin or Mr. Samuel Chotzinoff. Even in Scotland or Wales—countries in which one might maintain there is a quicker literary pulse than in the England of today—autobiographies are free of the rather ominous suggestion which often hangs about them in England: that they have been written because the writer could not get outside himself in order to write a novel or a poem.

And then, as I write, the exceptions spring to mind. If it is true that non-English writers like Mr. Sean O'Casey and Miss Margiad Evans have written memorably about themselves for no better reason than that they had a mind to, it is also true that the most ambitious autobiography of all is at the same time the most English. Sir Osbert Sitwell's *Left Hand, Right Hand!* is not only among the largest, it is also among the most beautifully planned of modern autobiographies. Cast in terms of sun and shade, of *lento* and *scherzo*, of stress and counterstress, it stands among the convincing monuments of our time. Like *Dichtung und Wahrheit*, it will not always be read straight through by its admirers of the future; they will take some passages at a run in order to linger over others. Yet they will agree, I believe, that Sir Osbert has done what he set out to do. He has created a poetic world within the world of a single lifetime. And while they applaud him I hope they will not forget to devote a little of their pleasure also to the enchanting book of his brother Sacheverell, *All Summer in a Day*. And then there is Mr. William Plomer's *Double Lives*. It is true that Mr. Plomer, like another excellent autobiographer,

Mr. Roy Campbell, can be claimed by South Africa as well as England, but *Double Lives* has a peculiar Bayswater tang about it. The merit of each of these books is somewhat similar. They are written by poets; they interpret a consistent view of life, and they are written with the kind of wit that often accompanies a keen sense of proportion.

Such are the autobiographies most likely to be remembered: books which not only summon back the past but do so with the authority of art. In the same category come *Olivia* and Lord Berners's *A Distant Prospect* and Sir Lawrence Jones's *A Victorian Boyhood*. It is still too early to speak of Mr. Richard Church's memoirs, since only *Over the Bridge* has appeared. But the evidence is already clear enough: Mr. Church, writing of his own childhood, speaks with a new authority. Our civilization may be ebbing away, these writers seem to assert in unison; the memorials of the future may be torn down as soon as they are built; but the past no-one can take from us. And here it is, exactly as we remember it: not always enjoyable, by no means closed to criticism, but entire and crystalline as the present is not.

This attitude I take to be a new one. People with long memories have always wished to preserve their records. They have written down for their grandchildren how they remember meeting an old gentleman who once danced with Marie Antoinette and another whose uncle had been a powder-monkey at Trafalgar. Others again have recorded with evocative skill—like Mr. Percy Lubbock in *Earlham*—the story of their home or the atmosphere of their boyhood. They have done so, however, with the air of someone adding to the continuous story of all civilized people. One more small tile has been fired and engraved and set in an unending wall. Now that attitude is changing. Memorialists are writing against time. They are putting things down as fast as they can, and they are asking for an immediate response —not the dilatory verdict of posterity.

That is why so many scarcely reach middle age before they launch into their memoirs. To name only some of the best: Mr. Spender, Mr. Lehmann, Mr. Harold Acton, Mr. Calder Marshall, Mr. Maclaren Ross: all of them are busy among their own records at an age when any earlier generation would have been squirreling away material, still only half-consciously, for a much later day. This is a matter which deserves a little investigation.

Take any writer (the autobiographies of non-writers must be looked at separately), and consider the alternatives open to him. He is 45, let us say, and he has a job which gives him a certain amount of free time. Yes, he is paid £1,800 a year by the B.B.C. He has a wife and three children, and out of all four he is extremely fond of two —not always the same two. He has published ten books, of which eight are forgotten. Twice he has been asked to contribute to highbrow papers in America. The British Council has sent him on more than one occasion to Belgium. He is asked to an inordinate number of publisher's cocktail parties, several First Secretaries invite him to luncheon and at least one Ambassador to dine. He owns a post-war car, and his shirts are cut to fit him, with the exception of one or two in a heavy green material which are reserved for addressing undergraduate clubs. In brief, he is a successful middle-aged writer who can pick his way through the world.

Private opinions? That is more difficult to arrange in a pattern. He had an evangelical childhood, and every

Sunday up to the age of nine he walked beside his father, without any particular sense of strain, to St. Michael's, Chester Square. His faith did not survive being prepared for confirmation by the headmaster, but ever since he has suffered occasional attacks of discomfort: a feeling of absence, of somebody in the next room. He has always meant to look up Kierkegaard, Pascal, Léon Bloy and Simone Weil in order to see if he can identify the exact presence, since foreigners seem to be more adept at the matter than the English (Lancelot Andrewes, just before the war, turned out to be a disappointing guide).

In politics he gave up conservatism when his father made a scene about some Cambridge bills. Sir Oswald Mosley's New Party did for a time, and he earned one of his first cheques for an article in *Action*. The Spanish War threw him into a dilemma. Not for the first time he found both sides unworthy of support, although the Anarchists held for him a certain charm. Modelling himself on Mr. E. M. Forster he finally decided to cultivate personal relationships, and carved out enough of them to promote three or four creditable novels and one divorce narrowly averted. The war of 1939 saved him from debt, and a slight knowledge of German from danger. Since being demobilized from one of the more secret parts of the Home Counties he has worked in Portland Place (once, Ovid-like, exiled for a year to Bush House) and consolidated a reputation the basis of which has already been forgotten by everyone.

Now he wants to launch off again. He cannot very well start with a novel, because personal relationships seem out of fashion in fiction, and they are all he knows about. He cannot write a Catholic novel, because he is not a Catholic, nor a satirical novel about life in a provincial university, because universities are already held in fee by a group of embattled dons who would certainly review him. There are travel-books of course, but the British Council has not sent him further than Belgium. Almost all other modern books seem to be about underwater fishing, mountain-climbing, the Esquimaux, or theology. In brief, there is nothing for it but an autobiography. And sure enough, as he reflects on the past, he finds himself much more interesting than he had supposed. Brave coloured patterns weave themselves out of the indiscipline of forty years, and a profound reluctance to throw away old letters turns out to be a god-send.

He is a gifted fellow, our writer, even though it is possible to pull his leg a little, yet his case is scarcely exaggerated. The most important thing about him is that, by 45, he has lost faith in his art and so in himself. The one thing he can do, therefore, is to write about that loss —in other words to write autobiographically. Mr. Connolly has said in effect that the purpose of writing is to produce masterpieces. No good writer, then, will be content merely to write. He will feel an increasing desolation as the years slip by. And it is one of the strange facts about our world that as its range extends so those aspects of the world worth writing about contract. More and more they bring the focal point of writing back to the human personality, as though by now we had astonished ourselves so deeply that we could make no further progress until we had sorted out the truth about the kind of people we really are.

Are we Progressives, for example, or religious maniacs, or hedonists, or do-gooders, or a generation living in the shadow of fear? Are we bored to death with public affairs, or hell-bent to abolish capital punishment, or soured scholars deprived by fate of access to a library? And if we are all these things simultaneously, can we trace no connecting links between our inconsistencies? If we cannot, we shall make no sense of our surroundings at all, and one day our schizoid tendencies will get the better of us. So for pity's sake—the argument goes—let us study ourselves before it is too late.

Our imaginary writer thus turns out to be a kind of Parsifal. Somewhere or other there is a Grail to be found (at 45 he will have read Jung as well as Freud) and if he looks closely enough into his heart he may stumble upon it. At any rate, that will be the last chance of justifying his gifts, of multiplying his talent. He may even consider that he is exploring one of the few fields of writing in which experiment is possible. Poetry and fiction and drama seem, for the time being, to have lost the art of self-renewal. But to write about oneself is to find some means of conveying a single unavoidable truth. The story-teller or the poet can modify their essence to suit their ends; they have multiple truths to command. The autobiographer has only one—much of it certainly discreditable—and the test of his technique is how much of it he can convey through the many-faceted cheat which is imposed upon him by every circumstance which hates or fears the truth.

Sometimes he may find it easier to talk about himself obliquely—not in the manner of Henry Adams, but under the disguise of fiction. Sir Harold Nicolson, in *Some People*, was among the first to exploit this device. And there are, for instance, the books of Denton Welch —where a radiant air of telling the truth is inseparable from the act of standing back a little, as if in order to see better. The truth of Denton Welch is a visionary truth, the vision wears a personal colour which stains everything upon which it falls. Here, perhaps, is one of the most striking justifications of the modern taste for self-discovery. For Welch was an invalid, his experience was forced inward, therefore, and it was gathered under the knowledge that he had not long to go. I conceive that a Victorian in similar circumstances might have remained silent for ever just because it did not occur to him to write of what he knew. As it is, we have been given a whole *oeuvre* singularly complete, unforced and particular. Had Welch lived to be 70, he could scarcely have added to the denseness and clarity which make him so memorable a writer.

On the whole, the reflective writers come out best of those who have felt impelled to set themselves down on paper. Adventures, for some reason, stale all too soon. Even the writers whom we remember in connection with the first World War are those of a poetic cast: Mr. Blunden, for instance, whose *Undertones of War* still shows how compulsive was the force which drove him to write it, or T. E. Lawrence. One might have expected the second war to make at any rate an equivalent impact on a younger generation. Somehow, it failed to do so. Indeed, of all the books which arose from direct experience of the fighting war, I can remember none which awakened much response in me, with the exception of Colonel Peniakov's *Private Army* and Mr. Douglas Grant's *The Fuel of the Fire*.

And yet I suppose that men in their middle years—in the years, that is, when the urge to write an autobiography is strongest nowadays—can have had no greater incitement than the war; nothing, in theory, can better have forced them to take stock of themselves than the ten years between 1937 and 1947—for the war was, of all wars, least confined to its duration. Yet in the event a kind of numbness seized us. The war of experience was already over before our own war began. Abyssinia and Spain and Austria and Czecho-Slovakia were the battlefields of the mind, and the real battlefields which followed later never touched the imagination half so closely. Indeed, for many of the more articulate British participants, the process of war, once experienced, was no more than an enormous and sometimes dangerous game of cops-and-robbers. The leaders pronounced noble words, but in the light of events whatever they said was greeted with the utmost cynicism by those who were actually doing the fighting. There was no question of disillusionment, because there had never been an illusion. The whole adventure seemed little except a vast interruption, so far as the lucky ones went, and a criminal farce played at the expense of the victims. Out of such thoughts not much that is memorable can arise. And so the innumerable personal stories of escape, of commando raids, of bombing and submarine warfare, pile up into heaps which have become anonymous. The stories may be good ones, but the *personae* scarcely count, except when a book is saved by the quality of its writing, as in *The Privileged Nightmare* by Mr. Giles Romilly and Mr. Michael Alexander, or Mr. John Verney's *Going to the Wars*.

In the background of such smaller experiences—if in the forefront of the time—stood, however, one overshadowing memorialist: Sir Winston Churchill. No comment, however brief, on the modern practise of autobiography can overlook the five volumes of what is, in effect, one of the most dramatic of personal stories. However they may come to be assessed as a history of the second World War they must keep an abiding interest for anyone concerned with the force of a human personality. For Sir Winston is doing what those in the battlefield generally failed to do: doggedly holding to an idea of what the war was about. Whether he was right or not is irrelevant to the success of his enterprise, in comparison with which all the memoirs of other public men of our time appear—according to their temperament—mild, narrow, or querulous.

One aspect of my subject seems to me quite inexplicable. The last ten years have seen a vast extension of the reading public; for many years previously, however, the process had been at work whereby money was being spread more evenly between rich and poor, education (in the widest sense) was carrying humane interests towards anyone with a bent for them, and the disabilities, as distinct from the realities, of poverty were being attacked one by one. Yet the writing of books remains an occupation of the middle and upper class. I do not speak of success stories: there are plenty of them. What lacks is any first-rate first-hand account of how practically everybody in the country is living from day to day. One can drive through Bromley and Liverpool and Dumfries with the surprising knowledge that there are no first-hand accounts to be had of what life has been like, for the last fifty years, in any of the little houses which line the streets. In fact, I can think of no character from real life who is so well founded in popular imagination as Mr. Pooter. Partly this must be because the inhabitants of everyday houses find everyday life extremely dull—or, if not dull, lacking in that special irritant which leads writers to write. But it is nevertheless odd that in a thickly-populated country no single exception should be discovered to the general rule that ordinary people (quite contrary to the evidence) believe themselves to be ordinary. There is, to be sure, a kind of book which exploits the ordinary with due skill. The books of Mrs. Robert Henrey fall into this class, and Mr. Bligh's *Tooting Corner* has carried skill into the realm of art. Yet the real life of the small streets requires a Goncourt or a Zola to pin it down with success—and of naturalists carrying so wide a spread of canvas we have none.

The artists and the Bohemians have not done so very much better. Mr. Augustus John, in *Chiaroscuro*, has snatched some brightly-coloured moments from oblivion, and Miss Nina Hamnett, in two books—of which *Laughing Torso* remains the more successful—has made a kind of *collage* out of some remarkable feats of memory. But when one looks into Mr. David Garnett's memoirs one is constantly arrested by the thought of the books that might have been, had the itch for autobiography only struck some of our writers and painters a little earlier in time. A fragment by Mr. Leonard Woolf sticks in the memory, but it does not touch the great days. Lord Keynes, Lytton Strachey, Francis Birrell: the list might be extended a long way. In one time and place a whole group of people lived much in one another's company, any one of whom was clearly born to be a memorialist, and all of whom were too discreet, or too occupied, to record the irreplaceable moments which ticked by. All we have been left is a certain number of published diaries— not least Virginia Woolf's—which still stir an echo of the kind of life for which English highbrows usually envy the French in vain. And here there is the promise of more to come. A whole covey of distinguished diarists is working in secret, we are told; on all hands the unprintable is waiting its day.

Such books might have made a refreshing contrast to a series of source-books which will be necessary to all students of English social life over the years before the war: the diaries of a confessed anti-highbrow, James Agate. These at any rate had a personal story to tell, even though they were bundled together without any idea of sequence other than a sequence in time. But for a really good account of what it was like to be a civilized, not too consciously highbrow, expert in the pleasures of living during the inter-war years I know no better book than one published under the name of George Vandon by the late Lord Derwent. It is called *Return Ticket*, and it is probably not much remembered today; for those in search of an intelligent period flavour and a cosmopolitan interest, it is, however, as fresh as the day it appeared.

There is one other kind of personal story which ought to be mentioned, since it belongs to a category which is peculiar to our times. This is the subjective travel book—the book which describes even more lovingly the journey towards a writer's heart than towards a traveller's destination. The best examples of such books are perhaps to be found among the works of Miss Freya Stark, but ever since, some twenty-five years ago, Mr. Peter Fleming wrote *Brazilian Adventure* and Mr. Julian Duguid *Green Hell* the personal travel-story has been much in fashion. There are Mr. Leigh-Fermor's *The Traveller's Tree*, Mr. Vincent Cronin's *The Golden Honeycomb*, Mr. Peter Mayne's *The Alleys of Marrakesh*, Mr. Laurie Lee's *A Rose for Winter*, Mr. Alan Ross's *The Bandit on the Billiard Table* and Miss Rose Macaulay's *Fabled Shore*, to name only half-a-dozen at random: books written with an objective purpose, certainly, but also in order to satisfy a need for self-definition.

It is not surprising that this should be so. The circumstances of our time have made travel unusually difficult and so confer a special prestige upon the individual who is able to break out of the lesser world of tourism. Not for nothing did Mr. Evelyn Waugh, a highly distinguished traveller of the 1930s, entitle a reprinted selection from his travel-writings *While the Going was Good*. And it has been a common experience that the act of travelling—to the Mediterranean basin above all—has enabled a whole tribe of writers, good and bad, to assuage their curiosity, not only about the face of the globe, but about themselves.

The difficulty in writing such notes as these is knowing when to stop. I have said nothing about a whole collection of books which I remember with vivid pleasure: Sir John Squire's *The Honeysuckle and the Bee*, Bishop Hensley Henson's *Retrospect of an Unimportant Life*, Sir Herbert Read's *Annals of Innocence and Experience*, Mrs. Blanche Dugdale's *Family Homespun*, Sir Robert Boothby's *I Fight to Live*, Mr. Edwin Muir's *An Autobiography* and so on. Nor have I attempted to draw any deduction from the whole assemblage of these tales. Are we more truthful than our ancestors? I think so. There is even a masochistic pleasure in the air; we like scoring off ourselves direct instead of punishing the characters in a fiction for our own faults. Are our lives more interesting? Yes, because we pay far more attention to unconsidered moments than our ancestors; we are more grateful for small mercies and less supine in our acceptance of people and things we dislike. Our nerves are tauter, yet at the same time we allow ourselves indulgences (and nearly all indulgences are good for writers) which earlier generations would have frowned upon. We still cannot speak the truth about our private lives, but we can hint. The handicap which offsets many of these advantages is, perhaps, that with all our additional freedom we are rather duller than our forebears. The scale of people diminishes as the scale of world events grows larger. Literature fills up with Cloughs and FitzGeralds. The Wordsworths, the George Eliots, the Ruskins, even the D. H. Lawrences, are lacking.

Before long, no doubt, the fashion will change once more. Writers will decide to be objective. They will feel towards the personal story that distaste with which today they regard the epic poem. That will come when the writers by vocation have discovered how to speak the truth about themselves, and so decide to move on, leaving autobiography to public men who hope to stave off oblivion.

Meantime, there is not a moment to be lost. The files are bulging with letters, the scribbled notebooks are all in order. If we do not get on with our own autobiography we may die and someone else will do the work for us, digging brutally into the tenderest part of our egos. To work, therefore; and in a year or two's time we shall find ourselves at our own publisher's party, holding a warm martini in one hand and extending the other to a very young woman who is asking, 'And did you actually *see* Aldous Huxley?' While, hurriedly trying to recall what we wrote we answer, 'Well, it's all a long time ago, but in those days I really knew him rather well. I remember one evening. . . .'

Twenty-five Years
of the Novel

———

FRANCIS WYNDHAM

———

How often has one heard the fact deplored, in discussions of English writing, that there are 'no young novelists', or, more accurately, no young novelists for whom a brilliant future can with any confidence be predicted? The difficulty of recognizing an enduring talent on the strength of one or two early books is so great that it is usually not admitted, and an assumption is made that the talent cannot exist. This embarrassing state of affairs does not, however, encourage reviewers of books and the intelligent reading public to caution; eager to spot a winner, they are now more than ever inclined to receive with joy a first book of any noticeable merit, and to over-praise it. No-one of literary pretensions can afford, in 1956, to mistake genuine originality for affectation or incomprehensible nonsense, and the magic word 'experimental' is often used to describe techniques that were in fact introduced more than thirty years ago and are now old enough to be respectable. The young writer today, if it is even suspected that there is a chance of his having anything to offer, can depend on a kind audience; but this position, apparently so satisfactory, has its roots in a profound pessimism and uncertainty. No-one is really convinced by the talk of new 'schools', of returns to some tradition or other, of dazzling debuts and exciting experimental work; most people secretly believe that there *are* no young novelists and, if pinned down, could at the best and with reservations name but one or two. And this is as it should be. Only rarely is a novelist born, self-contained and ready to be discussed, in his first book; apart from a few precocious exceptions, the novelist as a rule adds to his stature —and perhaps now and then diminishes it—gradually as the years go by; ironically enough, he may not win the particular form of recognition that definitely establishes him until he has published a book that is inferior to his earlier work but yet manages to bring his talent into focus.

Thus the careers of most novelists of worth are likely to conform to a prescribed cycle. For about ten years their books give pleasure to a comparatively small public; they are respectfully noticed by reviewers, but not yet firmly distinguished from their contemporaries; they do not go well at the lending libraries and are talked of with enthusiasm in avant-garde circles. Then, by a mysterious process, they become more widely known; perhaps an avant-garde admirer now works for a Sunday paper and has become an oracular figure; time has added weight to their reputations, they are seen to have stayed the course; the avant-garde admirers who have failed to get jobs on Sunday papers find themselves no longer members of a select band but (possibly to their annoyance) in accord with general opinion. A uniform edition is eventually published, earlier books which originally met with indifference are enthusiastically re-discovered, and the latest is a Book of the Month Club choice; pamphlets are written about them for the British Council, they may or may not agree to talk on the Third Programme and sit on literary committees, but if they do they speak with influence and authority. At the same time, a reaction has set in in certain quarters; the more intellectual reviews are likely to take up a slightly patronising attitude; those who loudly complained twenty years ago that such and such a writer was disgracefully neglected are now a little irritated that he is so widely enjoyed. His new books sell extremely well and are even sometimes made into films, but the general view is that they are less distinguished than his earlier work; that he is repeating himself, has nothing more to say and that success has made him complacent. He is now anything from forty to fifty, and when the English novel is discussed the cry goes up: 'Oh yes, we know all about *him*; but where are the *young* novelists?'

One wonders what would have been the answer to this question twenty-five years ago. 'We know now about D. H. Lawrence and E. M. Forster and James Joyce and Virginia Woolf and Wyndham Lewis and the brilliant young William Gerhardi and Aldous Huxley, just as once we knew about Wells and Bennet and Galsworthy and Somerset Maugham; but what of the future?' In 1931, the critic embarking on a prophetic article might well have mentioned Evelyn Waugh, for he could not have ignored the brilliance of *Decline and Fall* and *Vile Bodies*. He might have mentioned Rosamond Lehmann, who had followed her immensely popular *Dusty Answer* with a second novel, *A Note In Music*. Would he have spotted Elizabeth Bowen, who had published three novels and three volumes of stories but whose name was not

46

yet widely known? *Rumour At Nightfall*, the third novel
by Graham Greene, is unlikely to have impressed him
deeply; another third novel, I. Compton-Burnett's *Men
and Wives*, had possibly passed him by, and if he had
seen it his recommendation would probably be guarded.
He may easily have forgotten two recently published
first novels, L. P. Hartley's *Simonetta Perkins* and Christopher Isherwood's *All the Conspirators*; and Henry
Green's *Living*, though striking, presented some difficulties of syntax. If he had been shown in typescript
another first novel, Joyce Cary's *Aissa Saved*, shortly to
be published, his enthusiasm would presumably have
remained within bounds; on the other hand, he would
certainly have praised Anthony Powell's *Afternoon Men*,
while perhaps considering it rather too limited in range.
And it is certain that he would have named with confidence a number of people who are now either forgotten
entirely or whose talents have followed a course that is
plainly seen today as second-rate. But whatever his
answer, a sinister impression would have emerged from
it that young writers were mysteriously absent from the
literary scene.

Now that those writers who were there all the time
and are no longer young can be examined as a group, they
are seen to be a remarkably interesting collection who set
a dauntingly high standard for the young writer of today.
Not that the words 'group' and 'collection' apply to
them; as always, the best are fiercely individual, committed to no joint aim or shared view of the novel's
function. The least rewarding approach to the writers
just mentioned would be to compare them with each
other; the roads they follow are not the same, but neither
do they lead in opposite directions; some are nearer to-

gether than others, but all remain parallel and never meet. Mr. Waugh and Mr. Greene may both be converts to Roman Catholicism, but this fact alone cannot link them; Miss Bowen and Miss Lehmann have been loosely connected as head-mistresses in a school of feminine sensibility, but this is a confused and ignorant view which only high-lights, on examination, their differences; and Miss Compton-Burnett, Mr. Green and Mr. Cary are so single-minded in their originality that one imagines them as writing in a kind of void, superbly unaware of and utterly unaffected by what their colleagues are doing.

The artistic isolation of English novelists is worth emphasizing, as it is peculiar to this country, distinguishing the position here from that in France or in the United States. As is well-known, French novelists are taken, and take themselves, extremely seriously: they make pronouncements on political, religious and social controversies, often publishing their journals in which they reveal their relationships with each other, and the results of the competitions for the great literary prizes are awaited as eagerly as the results of sporting events or political elections. French writers are public figures to an extent that, in England, only Bernard Shaw and J. B. Priestley have equalled; and even here, more photographs appear in the popular press of Mlle Françoise Sagan, who has written two books, than of Miss Bowen or Miss Compton-Burnett. The publicity that surrounded the Existentialist movement is unthinkable in London; where is the café to which a tourist can be directed for a glimpse of Mr. Lehmann or Mr. Spender, when will a night-club be open called The Unquiet Grave? Similarly, intellectuals in America enjoy (or suffer from) a notoriety that includes details of their personal lives. American writers are easier to classify than English ones; in that country there is room for a Southern school to flourish, but here to be regional is to be unread. The public grants English intellectuals a privacy that is even denied the Royal family, and they use it to achieve an independence, not only of the public, but also of each other. They are comparatively lonely figures, and do not form a class; the very word 'intellectuals' has a meaning in other countries that does not apply here. If this solitude contains an element of pathos, it surely provides the best possible conditions for creative work while limiting the scope of criticism, which in England is likely to be tentative and dispersed, altogether less respectable an occupation than it is abroad. The result is satisfactory; more people read the creative writers than what is written about them, and a particularly dangerous form of literary inflation is avoided.

However, the creative writers must bide their time before they are read. The late George Orwell, for example, became widely celebrated after the publication of *Animal Farm* and *1984*; yet the author of slogans incorporated in the vernacular of the 'fifties belonged essentially to the 'thirties, and in fact remains an archetype of that era. Many others had reached the peak of their careers before 1940, and their fame since then has grown out of proportion to the value of their later work. Miss Compton-Burnett had written half her present output, setting herself a standard that she has consistently maintained, but not improved upon, as her public grows larger. Mr. Greene had written *The Power and The Glory*, for the first time dealing fully with a religious theme and adding a dimension to his talents;

E   49

since the war, he has twice elaborated on this theme, successfully with *The Heart Of The Matter* and less so with *The End Of the Affair*. Miss Bowen had written *The Death Of The Heart*; her post-war novels, *The Heat Of The Day* and *A World Of Love*, show mainly technical developments, though of impressive and sophisticated virtuosity, as do Miss Lehmann's *The Ballad And The Source* and *The Echoing Grove*. Mr. Henry Green and Mr. Isherwood had gone so far as to write their autobiographies, but while in Mr. Isherwood's case this was to prove a valedictory act—his best writing had been done in the 'thirties and the slight *Prater Violet* and the uncharacteristic and disappointing *The World In The Evening* were to add nothing to his achievement—Mr. Green was afterwards able to respond to the provocation of contemporary events. His next novel, *Caught*, is one of the few successful works of imagination inspired by the war, and his later comedies are unique in presenting an aspect of social life in post-war London. Mr. Cary shares with Mr. Green an uncanny gift for writing with equal success of totally different milieus, and he has also a subtle sense of the recent past; *The Horse's Mouth* may be his most popular work, but a case can be made out for the superiority of such earlier and more delicate novels as *Mr. Johnson* and *A House Of Children*. Mr. Powell had written five light and witty novels by 1940; the series on which he is at present engaged, begun after a long silence, deals with the period between the wars in a more leisurely and more ambitious manner. L. P. Hartley's *The Go-Between* was the big fiction success of 1953; how many of the people who enjoyed it realized that he had been writing, and writing well, since 1924? Mr. Hartley is yet another novelist who is happiest (as in his finest book, *The Shrimp And The Anemone*) when dealing with the past, and of those novelists at the height of their powers when war was declared only Mr. Green in *Caught* and Miss Bowen in *The Heat Of The Day* made serious attempts to approach the subject of war, both taking oblique roads towards it. Mr. Cary prefers to write of late-Victorian careerists, Mr. Hartley of Edwardian children, Mr. Powell of the '20s and '30s; and Mr. Waugh's dislike of the present is so apparent that whether he deals with aristocratic English families, early Christian saints, Californian cemeteries or army life, his world is as remote as that inhabited by Miss Compton-Burnett's impoverished and articulate landed gentry.

Meanwhile, those authors whose names were already made in 1930 continued to write. Somerset Maugham was among the most prolific, but he has never surpassed *Cakes And Ale*, which was published in that year. Both Wyndham Lewis and William Gerhardi are principally remembered for their work in the '20s, and it is possible that this will eventually be true of Aldous Huxley, who followed an unexpected path West towards an Eastern mysticism. On the other hand, Virginia Woolf added essentially to her art with her posthumous novel, *Between The Acts*, one of her finest and most important books. For many years Virginia Woolf exerted an influence over younger writers, with results that were often embarrassing; this is now, apparently, on the wane, and Wyndham Lewis, a writer long neglected, is increasingly discussed and, to some extent, even imitated. While the promising first novel of a few years ago was likely to aim at poetic sensibility and an allusive technique, its modern counterpart more often than not turns out to be a self-

consciously destructive satire, paying obsessive attention
to external details. Aldous Huxley cannot be called an
influential writer, as his own work is often an entertaining symposium of influences derived from varied
and unusual sources. E. M. Forster's long silence adds
urgency to his subtle message of humanism, and perhaps his influence may be discerned, in however oblique
a fashion, behind the spate of post-war novels designed to
prove that humanism is not enough.

Since 1940, of course, many new names have emerged.
Perhaps Patrick Hamilton should not, strictly speaking,
be counted among them; he was already well known
then as a playwright and slightly less so as a novelist; but
his two best books, *Hangover Square* and *The Slaves Of
Solitude*, came out during the 1940s and since then he
has embarked on a series of novels dealing with a criminal
called Gorse. These later books suffer from a repetitive
pattern imposed on them, but they are full of brilliant
detail, and though he sometimes spoils his effects by
facetiousness Mr. Hamilton is unsurpassed at conveying
the atmosphere of certain milieus typical of modern
English life and usually ignored in literature. Angus
Wilson, whose debut was among the most remarkable
of the post-war years, also eschews subtlety and fine
writing in his satirical studies of contemporary squalor,
but if Mr. Hamilton writes apparently with the detachment of a social historian Mr. Wilson, inspired by
moral indignation, creates a nightmare world of his own
in which aspects of real life are exaggerated and distorted. Both these writers, in their exuberant humour,
owe something to Dickens, and Mr. Wilson has made
public his admiration for Zola. Such influences were
unusual at a time when Henry James was being enthusi-

astically reinstated, and the examples of E. M. Forster and Virginia Woolf were still followed; to some extent they forestalled a later, and more self-conscious, reaction against the psychological novel involving the work of William Cooper, Kingsley Amis, John Wain, Iris Murdoch and others. These gifted young writers have published some successful comedies in which the heroes' gaucherie lands them in amusingly uncomfortable situations. By implication, however, the gaucherie itself is a likeable quality, in contrast to the prevalent pretentiousness with which these heroes are surrounded. The comic formula is entertaining, but already in danger of becoming stale with repetition; the seedy backgrounds lack Mr. Hamilton's uncanny accuracy and the boisterous satire could do with some of Mr. Wilson's feline point. However, an implied aggressiveness on the part of Mr. Amis and Mr. Wain was responsible for a brief and enjoyable squabble, in the correspondence columns of literary reviews, between the 'red-brick University' school and the upholders of metropolitan culture: two cliques were assumed to exist, the one accused of cockiness and provincialism, the other of snobbishness and artistic anaemia. Nobody took this very seriously, but the artificiality of the wrangle was significant, proving that the literary scene of the early 1950's contained so hungry a need for sensation that the first bright newcomers to appear on it must enter with, and be received by, an unnecessarily militant spirit.

This need was no doubt caused by the independence, already mentioned as a characteristic of good English novelists, shown by those whose reputations were made since 1940. A typically lonely figure was Denton Welch, whose novels were distilled from his own distinctive personality and experiences. They were sustained by the curious toughness that a minor, delicate and limited talent can sometimes have—that, for example, Katherine Mansfield's had. Destined like Katherine Mansfield to die in his early thirties, his art reached a precocious maturity as hers did, and his posthumous novel, *A Voice Through A Cloud*, is as likely to survive as anything published since the war. William Sansom, too, evades easy classification; his work is remarkable chiefly for a dazzling verbal virtuosity, and in his best book, *The Body*, he directed his own poetic vision on to Patrick Hamilton territory, with fine results. His novels since then, however, have been little more than animated travel-books, skilfully done but lacking the imaginative quality of his early writing, and apparently addressed to a less demanding public. He illustrates the truth that travel, while possibly broadening a novelist's mind, can have an opposite effect on his art. Totally different, again, is the work of C. P. Snow, who has steadily and unostentatiously made a unique position for himself over the last fifteen years or so. His books are reminiscent, at least superficially, of Arnold Bennet, some of Wells and Maugham's *Of Human Bondage*. They are not distinguished by fine writing, poetry or wit, but concentrate on a sober exposition of human character. They reflect a balanced sense of moral values and an intelligent breadth of interest: the theme is often the making of a career in the modern world. Rooted in a masculine conception of the novel's function, they continue a neglected tradition and are less immediately attractive than the more frivolous or more pretentious work of some of his contemporaries.

Many of the novelists mentioned above have also

worked within the more vaguely defined, but no less demanding, frame of the short story, and while in most cases the results have been enjoyable footnotes to their longer work, some have added considerably to its scope. Elizabeth Bowen, for example, has written many short stories as brilliant as her novels, and the talents of James Stern, H. E. Bates, Denton Welch, William Sansom and Angus Wilson are particularly well suited to this form. Probably the best short stories written today, however, are those by V. S. Pritchett, who shares with Henry Green, Joyce Cary and Patrick Hamilton an outstanding gift for reproducing vernacular.

Dialogue plays an important part in modern English writing, often carrying overtones and undertones of extreme subtlety that must surely be lost in translation, and in some cases treated in a highly stylized and personal way. Miss Compton-Burnett's conversation is as mannered as Meredith's, Mr. Green's as allusive as Kipling's, Mr. Hamilton's as eccentrically idiomatic as Dickens', and Miss Bowen's (in her later books) as tentative as Henry James'. Henry Green has even suggested that the novel today should consist almost entirely of dialogue, obliquely unfolding the narrative in a succession of hints, approximations, exaggerations and understatements, as drama so often manifests itself in real life. Certainly such subtle writers as Mr. Green himself, Elizabeth Bowen, Anthony Powell, and Joyce Cary seem to demand an alertness, even a faculty of intuition, in their readers, that is unnecessary for appreciation of (for example) a book by Graham Greene, where the narrative has the speed and clarity of a film and the complexity lies in the situations described. Mr. Greene has his subject—intimately connected with his religious faith—

which can be approached directly and its intricacies analysed; Miss Bowen, Mr. Powell and Mr. Green, widely different from each other as they are, work their way towards a truth—in the first case, about emotion, in the second, about society, in the third, about both—in a tentative spirit that enriches their writing with personal allusions and necessitates an original technique. Such sophisticated writers are sometimes accused of placing more importance on method than content, of being 'writer's writers'; and certainly a degree of virtuosity can be reached where the subject is in danger of appearing trivial in contrast to its treatment. Yet how dull and pedestrian the worthy, talented and impersonal novel can seem beside the work of the virtuosos!

At almost every period in the history of the modern novel, there is to be found an impressive number of young women capable of producing clever, tasteful and enjoyable books. At present, two stand out as certain to sustain their already considerable accomplishment: Olivia Manning and Elizabeth Taylor. Mrs. Taylor's writing bears some resemblance to Elizabeth Bowen's, and the influence is for good; Miss Manning, also intelligent, sensitive and witty, is unusually successful at writing about men, and has more than once chosen a male character as her protagonist. Each has half a dozen good books to her credit, most of them written during the last ten years. These writers have long passed the stage of promise; but every year first or second novels appear by women who may later establish themselves in this happy position and who more often than not fail to stay the course. On the other hand, a select number of women novelists are able to make a distinguished place for themselves with one or two books of unusual merit. Julia Strachey is one of these:

she has published two very short novels and a handful of stories, but her name should be mentioned in any survey of original contemporary writing. The late Jean Rhys was another, whose bitter and brilliant *Good Morning, Midnight* and *Voyage In The Dark* are too little known. Perhaps Stevie Smith, author of the unique and unrepeatable *Novel On Yellow Paper*, belongs in this exclusive group. For many years Antonia White remained in it, admitted on the strength of her early *Frost In May*; she has lately broken her silence with a trilogy, of great interest but less artistically perfect than the first book.

But what of the younger men? They seem to take longer to get under way. P. H. Newby, J. D. Scott, Ernest Frost . . . their work is civilized, accomplished, not yet quite individual—although Mr. Newby's last novel, *The Picnic At Sakhara*, showed that he had finally found the right note for himself. Robert Kee, who has written twice about the war and once about the future, is evidently a born novelist; scenes in these admirable novels hint that he could excel, if he chose, at a genre other than the semi-documentary or the semi-thriller. Jocelyn Brooke, who wrote two impressively morbid short novels, has now abandoned this form for the cosier one of fictionalized autobiography. Nigel Dennis' *Cards Of Identity* was highly admired, William Golding has published two remarkably original novels, Chapman Mortimer is interesting mainly for his style (how refreshing to find a young writer who can be accused of being precious), Hugo Charteris and Thomas Hinde have written first novels of unusual promise . . . but to continue with a catalogue of names is invidious, misleading, and comparatively pointless: the crystal ball remains cloudy.

One reason for its obscurity is that the general standard
of novel writing in England is far higher now than it has
ever been before. This is unexpected, as novel-writing
has ceased to be a specialized pursuit; the professional
field has been confusingly over-run with amateurs.
Everybody, it used to be said, has a book in them; nowadays, everybody seems to write it, and more often than
not it turns out to be a novel. Presumably the submerged production and consumption of trash increases
with the population, but the average lending-library
novel of today is likely to be more intelligent and accomplished than its counterpart in the past. In the 1930s, one
could be fairly certain that an 'ordinary' French novel
would be better written than its English equivalent, and
second-rate American novelists seemed to possess a gift
of readability rarer in this country. This is no longer so
today, when the yearly number of praiseworthy, if
undistinguished, English novels is gratifyingly high. The
fact that the general standard of entertainment has been
raised is sometimes deplored as coinciding with, and
mysteriously responsible for, an absence of 'giants';
certainly it makes the giants less easy to recognize at the
early stages of their growth. Articles appear more and
more frequently with such titles as 'Is the Novel dead
as an art form?' and this loss of faith in the vitality of
fiction seems to have been prompted by the fact that
more and more people are able to produce it, in an
acceptable form. Surely, this being the case, the novel
can seldom have been more alive? I timidly suggest,
admitting the possible absence both of giants and of
brilliant newcomers, that it is nowhere more alive than
in England. The mere fact that our most eminent novelists are individual and isolated figures, without disciples

and imitators, who make rules for themselves but not for their colleagues, who ignore fashion but respect tradition and pose neither as instigators nor as destructive agents, is a healthy sign for the future. There is no organized front to react against, so we shall be spared the tedious excesses of revolt; no self-conscious school, either moral, political or stylistic, so we shall be spared the barrenness of imitation. The new generation will emerge gradually as their predecessors have done, and may possibly be met with even more encouragement. Now in England it is easy to be published, easy to be read, no more difficult than it has ever been to make money by the pen, and just a little more difficult than formerly to add anything of significance to the scope of a form that, though young, has developed with precocious speed.

Experiment and the Future
of the Novel

PHILIP TOYNBEE

T HE WORDS 'EXPERIMENT' and 'experimental' have been too freely and yet too narrowly applied to the novel. A book which is printed upside down, or in particoloured print, can still be acclaimed in some parts of Europe as a bold and interesting experiment, even if its matter is the most hackneyed imitation of Molly Bloom's soliloquy or *Les Chants de Maldoror*. The reason for this confusion of terms seems to be twofold. In the first place the word 'experimental' has come to be applied only to novels which appear to be making an experiment in method. In the second place even experiments in method are usually taken for granted and accepted quite quickly, provided that they have obviously succeeded. This leads us to assume that the methodologically experimental novel is a new phenomenon of which the first exponents were Joyce, Virginia Woolf and Kafka. Even Proust, whose experiments in method were perhaps the most successful of anyone's in this century, is no longer thought of as experimental.

Indeed one might perhaps say that the more thoroughly successful a novelist's new methods have been—

in the sense of their wide and general acceptance on the main highway of subsequent fiction—the more quickly his original contribution has been forgotten. Joyce remains for us the prototype of the experimental novelist simply because very few of the new methods which he evolved have proved to be capable of exploitation by his successors. This is not to say, of course, that Proust is therefore a greater novelist than Joyce, but it is to say that he has proved a more fertilizing one. It was not conceivable that any later novelist could progress further than *Finnegan's Wake*, any more than later writers have ever progressed further than *The Anatomy of Melancholy* or than the novels of Ronald Firbank. Such works as these are like buffers at the ends of particular railway sidings, but this does not prove that they were more original, even in method, that those other books which have laid down a further stretch of the main line.

If we remain aware both that novelty of method is quickly forgotten once the new method is accepted, and also that there are many other kinds of novelty, then we may begin to wonder whether any great novelist has ever been unexperimental. Indeed this doubt quickly turns into the frustrating awareness of a truism if we ask ourselves whether any great novelist of the past has ever failed to do anything new at all. In that direction, though I believe that the logical progress is reasonable enough, there lies a danger of destroying distinctions for the sake of a literal use of language. Not a book has ever been written, even by the most ardent of plagiarists, which was not new at least by a few changes of vocabulary and punctuation. Common-sense comes to our aid when we reflect that there is, nevertheless, a very real distinction to be made between a novelist like Fielding and one like

61

Richardson, between a Jane Austen and a Dickens, a
Thomas Hardy and a Henry James. Both groups presented new and impressive visions of the world but,
while the second group were consciously possessed by
their novelty of vision, the first were far less aware that
what they were doing was something new.

The distinction is a vague one, a debatable question of
emphasis, but if we refuse to make it we are left without
a distinction where one is obviously required. Kafka
wrote simple narratives in a simple form, and his books
could be read as fairy-stories by an intelligent and
melancholic child. We agree in calling him experimental not because of any novelty of method, in a narrow
sense, but because he explored a new fictional dimension.
A new physical dimension was explored by St. Exupéry,
and this might seem a comparatively trivial form of
novelty if the writer had not discovered a new vocabulary
to deal with his new material. Lawrence, though firmly
assured of his traditionalist role by the labours of the
Cambridge school, foisted a new idea on us and found a
new instrument for doing so. Miss Elizabeth Bowen has
presented us with a new sensibility and a new form of
feminine intelligence. Yet somewhere along this line
our distinction must lie, for it is as clear that Miss Bowen
is not what we mean by an experimental novelist as that
Kafka is precisely one of the things that we do mean by
it.

If we were examining here the past practice of novelists it would be useful and interesting to follow the line
of enquiry which was begun thirty years ago by Mr.
Percy Lubbock. It would be possible to examine in detail
the methods which have succeeded each other and to
penetrate by way of method into a critical examination

of the word in all its aspects. But what is not possible is to discuss *the future* in such terms. Any predictions about method which I myself could make would be no more than predictions about the way in which I myself shall hope to write novels. It is the nature of each new development in method that it had not been predictable until it was made, and a discussion of the future in terms of first and third persons, streams of consciousness, author's omniscience and the rest would be to indulge in a very empty discussion indeed. For the truth is that an examination even of past method is of no general interest unless it is used as a means of discussing the infinitely more important elements which lie behind method. No important novelist of the past, with the possible exceptions of Flaubert and Joyce, has elevated method to a parity of consideration with those proper though vague masters of method which we describe as vision, perception, moral value, order, imagination, truth. . . . We know all about the inseparability of method from these other elements which lie behind it, but if we are critics we had better beware of knowing too much about it. It is our job to make these distinctions, even if we try to obliterate them afterwards, and the simple distinction which I would make is that the 'how to do something' must be subordinate in the serious writer's mind to the 'what to do' and the 'why to do' it. Indeed the 'why to do' it, which seldom exercises the minds of critics, seems often to loom largest of all in the minds of despondent writers.

Why, then, should an Englishman of 1956 try to write a serious novel? We must dismiss the lyingly cynical answers just as we must dismiss, for *this* enquiry, the temptingly general ones. We must not suppose that he *merely* wants to make money or a name for himself, and we must not be content to say that he wants to express himself. Why does he want to write a novel *now*? And the answer must surely be that it is because he believes that he has understood something about our present condition which has not been expressed by anybody else. The answer may seem a flat one at first, for it might be said that this was always the intention of the serious novelist and that there is nothing new in it. But what is, I believe, comparatively new in the answer I have given is the insistence on the words 'our present condition'. Whatever may be said in favour of or against our own time it is clearly not one of those periods from which we can respectably or naturally dissociate ourselves. The comparatively 'timeless' novels of the past, like *Wuthering Heights* or *Dominique* or all the novels of Jane Austen, were always the exceptions. They have now become an impossibility. The enormous figure of 'the times' has filled the novelist's horizon more and more, and every effort to elude it becomes more and more artificial, strained and improper. Proust, Joyce, Virginia Woolf—these were perhaps the last important novelists who were able, without discredit to themselves and to their work, to treat their times as no more than a convenient vehicle. Even Proust was possessed by his own times to the extent that social signs of them became one of his major themes. We are dealing again in a distinction which is as impressive as it is real for it could easily be said that no novelist has ever written who was not perceptibly influenced by the period in which he lived. Yet the distinction becomes real again if we contrast Dickens with Jane Austen or Zola with Hardy.

Much was done—much is still being done—to distort

this insistence on the novelist's present obligation to be concerned with the situation of his times. The Marxists have interpreted this just, and justly vague, insistence as a demand that writers should deal with certain specific subjects in a specific tone and with specific recommendations. The Flaubertians, misinterpreting their master as the Marxists seem to have misinterpreted theirs, make a similar assumption. They believe that if we indulge our natural compassions, our natural fears, our natural hopes as creatures of our time, then we shall be condemned to writing the kind of novels which the Marxists recommend.

But what can and must be said about the times is that we are all associated with one another as never before and that every individual, liking this or loathing it, is bound to the community by stronger bonds than ever before. The hydrogen bomb is simply the most powerful and alarming symbol of this new association, which has, of course, its many positive and generous aspects as well. It is still possible in England for a few very rich or very private-minded or very ascetic individuals to imitate a Montaigne or a Flaubert and to live as if they were immune from the virus of society. But it is surely most unlikely that anyone can now do this without being perpetually aware of his unnatural action, and perpetually aware, as well, of the very society which he is trying so hard to escape. In our time nobody talks so much about the modern world as those many modern intellectuals who busily denounce it and volubly lament the passing of better days. I am not saying at the moment that I think it morally wrong to try to escape from the world and from our fellow-creatures—though I do think this: I am saying that it can no longer be done without a self-consciousness which is ultimately stultifying to the writer. Even Flaubert, making his own retreat a hundred years ago, was so obsessed by his hatred of the bourgeois whom he was supposedly avoiding that his writing talent was perceptibly distorted.

. The misinterpretation of this demand that the modern novelist must be *concerned* springs from the absurd demand that he must also be *engaged*. We have watched, and many of us with some disgust, the progress of an engagement in the person of Jean-Paul Sartre. When he emerged from the war with the slogan of engagement on his lips he was clearly determined to distinguish this demand from the old, crude and lethal doctrine of the Communist culture bosses. Today his notion of engagement differs scarcely at all from theirs. Engagement demands that the novelist should be left-wing, and preferably communist in his views; that he should expound such views in his novels; that he should write the novels in a spirit of hatred for those whose politics are different and of admiration for the working classes; that his books should be intelligible to those who are totally uneducated in the history and development of the novel. These are murderous demands and since they were first promulgated some thirty to forty years ago no single novel of value has complied with them.

Concern is a far harder thing to define, which may lead us to suppose, in a field where so much is indefinable, that it is a far better thing to pursue. Once again it can be illustrated more easily than it can be described. I will tentatively say that Proust, Joyce, Firbank and Virginia Woolf were comparatively unconcerned in the sense I mean; that Gide, Mauriac, Lawrence, Malraux and Faulkner were all, in their totally different ways, deeply

66

concerned. The first group is not to be reproached for this reason. They are the novelists of yesterday, and of a yesterday when the demand for this kind of concern could not be made with any authority. I am writing here about today and tomorrow. Now and in the immediate future it seems to me that some kind of intimate concern for the present situation of ourselves, our neighbours and our society, must be felt by the serious novelist. To write today in the spirit of Firbank would be a literary offence, for it could not be done without triviality.

It will be seen from the list of concerned novelists which I have just given that the quality of concern can be accompanied by widely different views, can reveal itself through widely different material, can be given shape and expression by widely different methods. One of the greatest and most deeply-concerned novels of our time was Thomas Mann's *Joseph and his Brethren*, a book which was set in the fourteenth century B.C. Mauriac writes about a narrowly regional bourgeoisie, and writes about them from a point of view which is certainly alien to the elusive 'spirit of the times'. Malraux's best novel was about Chinese peasants, while Faulkner chooses for his subject one of the most decayed and obsolete sub-classes in the world. Similarly Gide and Faulkner used new methods in their novels, while Lawrence and Mauriac were content with old ones.

Is there, then, any relationship at all between the two subjects I have been discussing, between the two distinctions which I have tried to draw? Is there a relationship between concern on the one hand, novelty of vision, material, tone or method on the other? By almost all the apparent evidence there is none. Indeed if there is any such relationship it might easily be supposed that a certain traditionalism in technique and material might more readily be combined with a strong and immediate concern for the state of the world. Concern, it might be said, will imply that the writer wishes to be widely read and understood, so that he may the better and more quickly come to the help of that wide community which engages his compassion. But this, I believe, is to slip at once across the line which divides concern from engagement. For concern does not for a moment imply that the writer who is possessed of it should use his novels for any specific purpose. Of course he hopes that his books will have an effect on the minds and feelings and perceptions of his readers: he hopes to show them something that he has seen, thought, felt, and he hopes that they will be altered, however minutely, by these revelations. But the desire that these readers will act, in any public sense, differently after reading him is a naive and arrogant desire which only an engaged idiot would indulge. Concern, though this may sound a harsh and contradictory thing to say, is better viewed as a gift to the writer than as any ready advantage to the majority of readers. And for this reason it would be absurd to recommend that a writer should show or feel more of it than he does. He will feel it or he will not, according to his nature as a human being.

But I believe that we can say something more than this. I believe we can say that the modern English novelist who is deeply concerned about his fellows and his society will also be concerned with new methods, new ideas, new sensitivities and new material. He will belong, in his compassion and responsibility, to the tradition of Dickens, George Eliot and Conrad. He will belong, in his conscious ambition to see and express things newly, to the tradition of Henry James, Joyce and Virginia Woolf.

These assertions may seem arbitary, and it is true that they are founded on little more than a sense of private fitness, a private hope for the future rather than any clear evidence from the present. In fact there would seem just now to be a notable separation of these two traditions. We are often told that the better young novelists in England are at least agreed that the day of the experimental novel is over. We are further told that the majority of them write more in the spirit of Sartre's Nauseated Man than of Robert Elsmere. It might seem, in fact, that their common aim is to express in an old way the fact that they have no feeling and no vision at all.

This has been suggested, but I do not for a moment believe that it is true. In the pundit's article from which I extracted this interpretation of the modern scene Mr. Kingsley Amis was quoted as an example of this composite tendency. But it seems to me that Mr. Amis, a lively, talented and successful young novelist, exhibits precisely the opposite combination of attributes and intentions. He is concerned in the most obvious sense and, though there is nothing new in his method, he is consciously and delightedly dealing with new material, consciously and delightedly applying his new vision to the new world which he has discovered. Mr. Chapman Mortimer, a very different kind of novelist and an older one, applies to his characters a wholly new vision and a new vocabulary. He is concerned in the simple sense that he is compassionate, but his books are deliberately set in a world which has very few temporal or spatial points of reference. There is a group of young men and they are somewhere in Paris and the time is approximately the present. But Mr. Mortimer's great merit as a novelist lies, as did Henry Green's before him, in seeing the world afresh, in discovering for himself a new and surprising perch from which to view the behaviour of human beings. If Mr. Amis is more concerned than he is new, Mr. Mortimer is more new than he is concerned. But between them these two newcomers to the English novel represent the two kinds of development which will, I believe, eventually coalesce.

To find a satisfactory example of this coalescence I have had to go to America, and the best modern example I know of a novel which combines a concern for the modern world with a conscious attempt to do something new is Salinger's *The Catcher in the Rye*. This hauntingly comic and sad story about a truant high-school boy shows a double compassion of author for hero and hero for all his associates. Indeed by the end of that book that astonishing hero has become an almost dostoievskian figure, a Myshkin or Alyosha who carries his quaint cross through a seedy New York instead of through a seedy provincial Russia. At the same time the book is undoubtedly new-minted both in method and outlook. There was nothing new in writing a first-person narrative in dialect, but there was something new and startling in accepting *this* dialect. For the hero's language is the almost inarticulate argot of American adolescence—precisely the kind of language which is held up for angry ridicule by those who spend their time in abusing the modern world. There is nothing rich or racy about the idiom which Mr. Salinger had boldly chosen—nothing of Mark Twain's Mississippi or Hardy's Wessex. It reads— and I am assured that the idiom is accurate—like the dying fag-end of a language, a clotted and half-dumb perversion in which almost nothing can be said with vigour or clarity.

Yet it is through this medium—for Salinger never steps outside it—that ideas and sentiments of the most gentle subtlety are purveyed to us. It is true that *The Catcher in the Rye* is a tour-de-force—by which I mean that it has the marks of a single brilliant achievement carried out against all the odds. But some such wrestling against odds, some such deliberate defiance of the easy option seems to me to be almost an obligation to the modern novelist. This, I take it, is approximately that quality of 'terrorism' which Jean Paulhan defined for us in his *Fleurs de Tarbes*—an attitude of the writer to his material which certainly resembles that of a wrestler towards his opponent rather than that of an exquisite lady playing with her jewels or of a leisurely gentleman walking along a street.

I am moving here towards the more specific subject of method, though I have earlier warned myself against treating it too specifically. What I am saying is that it is no longer possible to write a good book in the manner either of Max Beerbohm or of Trollope, of Logan Pearsall Smith or of Arnold Bennett. The natural fine writing of Beerbohm is no longer available to us since there is no longer a social group in which fine talking is natural. There is plenty of good and vigorous conversation in many social groups, but it does not take an exquisite or cadenced form. And it is clear to anyone who has ever thought about the subject that a literary language which is unrelated to any spoken language quickly becomes an impossibility. The language which Beerbohm used for his writing was not, of course, the same as the language which he and his friends used in their conversation. But it was related to the natural language of talk as a balloon in the air is related to a balloon on the ground. We no longer have *that* balloon on the ground with us.

On the other hand the easy and acceptably pedestrian manner of Trollope and Bennett is no longer available to us either. For this depended on a norm of ordinary educated speech which still possessed just sufficient energy and freshness to make it a possible basis for a literary language. Such a norm still exists, but it has grown so stale and unprofitable that no lively or even genuinely conscientious writer can do anything with it. This is the point which is always missed by those critics who insist that the only good style is a plain style, and that the best way to say something in prose is the most straightforward way. To be plain in the manner of our modern plainness is simply to be hackneyed and inexpressive.

So the concerned novelist of our day cannot, in any obvious sense, be a plain writer, and he cannot, in any previous sense, be a gem-like writer. I do not know what he can be, though I like to think that I am finding my own private way through this dilemma. And that is surely the point about the English novelist's position today and in the immediate future—that he is on his own, struggling in a collapsed tradition, uncertain of his intractable medium and uncertain of his constantly changing material. Every battle fought with a book has to be a battle fought with new weapons on a new battlefield. The modern novelist is indeed supported by recent and magnificent examples, for the first thirty years of his century were the richest in all the short history of the novel. But the last quarter of a century has transformed his society, transformed his language, transformed his intellectual and emotional climate. While he has been forced, as a human being, into a more intimate relationship with his society, as a writer he has been forced into greater isolation. There is no longer any obvious material or obvious method; there is no longer a fruitful form of plain talking or a fruitful body of accepted ideas. Each new novelist must now make every decision for himself, unlike the majority of past novelists for whom much had been decided without their knowledge. The temptation, then, is to look for a total privacy which shall place the human being in a state of voluntary isolation to match the involuntary isolation of the writer. But I have suggested that this cannot be achieved without a distortion of the human being which must have the effect of distorting the writer too. To live in isolation today—and I do not mean to live in a light-house but to live in emotional aloofness—is a more unnatural action than it has ever been before. To write in anything but isolation is impossible, since the act of trying to write a serious novel is a more lonely exploration than it has ever been before. The outlook, in fact, is harsh and stimulating.

73

Poetry:
Tradition and Belief

—

ROY FULLER

—

'ICANNOT SEE THAT poetry can ever be separated from something which I should call belief', T. S. Eliot remarked in 1927, going on to explain that by 'belief' he did not necessarily mean orthodox or unorthodox Christian belief, nor, indeed, religious belief at all. The pulse of English poetry since those words were written can be measured against the ability of the individual poet or group of poets to find an attitude of mind of sufficient confidence not only to draw into poetry a massive subject matter but also to envisage a real audience and find a proper voice. Putting a few years of poetry under a magnifying glass means seeing the question of 'belief' in all its crudity—naiveté, timorousness, rashness in the face of outward events, an easy response to fashions and false prophets. But it is the accumulation of these quite simple reactions which in retrospect gives a period its density of tone and determines the quality of its successes, the depth of its failures.

Poets who have successively emerged from their youth since 1914 have usually felt their greatest problem to be one of belief. No doubt a minority has accepted Christianity or Marxism: accepted, that is to say, a dogmatic ideological system to be worked out in poetry. But most have inherited the vague and difficult humanism of the Western World, and even those nominally Christian or socialist (or both) have not often found their dogmas of sufficient vigour to dictate the attitude of their verse. At the moment this humanism, confronted with the special phenomena into which the general problem of a growing industrial civilization has crystallized—the revolutions in the East, the growth of state control in the West, atomic weapons, the struggle for colonial freedom, the partition of the world—finds it hard to take a moral attitude. Its feelings are ambivalent, its comments choked; and the poetry arising out of it is not able—probably does not desire—to do more than share with a few others its dubieties or cynicisms about the age, the consolations of nature or personal love.

> *Born between wars*
> *I missed the golden age*
> *When art and action fused*
> *Into a single voice.*

This is the start of a poem called *Neutrals* by Philip Oakes, one of the more interesting of the newest poets, and perhaps 'neutralism' is a convenient term for the typical absence of belief characteristic of his generation. But most neutralists, though finding their neutralism inevitable, feel it to be an unsatisfactory poetic position, and the reason is not hard to find.

In one sense the problem of belief has haunted English poetry since the Industrial Revolution. The decline of the powers of Wordsworth and Coleridge coincided with the growth of their neutralism: Shelley's great output was stimulated and articulated by the comprehensive

75

system of Godwinism: Tennyson and Arnold are troubled at the centre of their poetry by their perception that, as the latter poet said, 'the past is out of date, the future not yet born'. From our own times we see in the eighteen nineties and the nineteen twenties the cul de sac of art for art's sake, and admire the best poetry of the First World War and the nineteen thirties as arising out of an age 'when art and action fused'.

This relationship between modern poetry and the philosophical or political conceptions of its period is obviously far from simple. It is not, for example, that poetry to be healthy needs to be didactic but rather that the individual poet has usually found it beyond his power to link poetry to life, to incorporate life in his poetry, through his own unsupported efforts. And in the ideological and cultural state of the modern world the poet has found it more and more difficult to come by support of the kind which will enable him to go on writing poetry. The age is political but the poet in general feels himself outside politics: the crucial experiences of mankind rise from events on the political, the social level, but the poet often feels himself outside society. These contradictions have led some poets and critics to deny the need for the poet to be more than a sensitive medium. I. A. Richards, for instance, has said (in *Science and Poetry*) that 'experience is its own justification'.

What follows assumes that experience *qua* experience cannot sustain a great nor for long even a satisfactory poetry, that without a vision of life which includes the power of criticizing society and a belief in the social function of art, poetry is always in danger of degenerating into triviality, stock response, dead forms. But I shall try to look at the poetry of the present and the immediate past not as an expression of ideology or lack of it—for such a viewpoint tends to introduce irritations arising from the ideological quirks of both critic and reader. Poetry is first of all a matter of language and technique and it is this aspect I wish mainly to discuss, though I hope to show how intimately these things are connected with belief. I shall not attempt to define 'belief' any more closely than Eliot did on the occasion I quoted at the outset, but leave it to be seen as the shadowy but compelling presence over every poet's shoulder.

2

The main characteristic of our verse in this century is the distinction between the diction and the *raisons d'être* of poetry which have lingered on from the previous period and those inaugurated by the poetic revolution of the second decade of the century. That this truism needs still to be stated is shown by a recent anthology under distinguished auspices, *The Faber Book of Twentieth Century Verse*. Its introduction discussed the verse of the period in classifications which cut across the great distinction I have mentioned—dividing it, for example, into such unmeaningful categories as verse of Innocence and Experience, of the Garden and the City. The collection which resulted accordingly failed to indicate the peculiar triumphs of the poetry of our time: indeed, by diluting it with work in an outworn tradition it tried to sanction that eclectic view of verse against which the best poets and critics of the century have always struggled.

The change in the diction and motives of poetry characteristic of the century is perhaps best understood by considering a number of streams of varying size which by the end of the twenties, say, had become an irresistible flood. The most important contribution came from Eliot, as worked upon by Pound. Eliot's influence exerted itself in several ways. As a critic he had noted the virtues of English poetry up to the arrival of Milton, when truly bad verse could scarcely be written, and he described and evaluated the two periods in singularly persuasive terms: 'Tennyson and Browning are poets, and they think; but they do not feel their thought. . . . A thought to Donne was an experience; it modified his sensibility. . . The poets of the seventeenth century, the successors of the dramatists of the sixteenth, possessed a mechanism of sensibility which could devour any kind of experience . . . In the seventeenth century a dissociation of sensibility set in, from which we have never recovered'. Eliot carried his high valuation of sixteenth- and seventeenth-century poets into his own early practice as a poet. Unafraid of wit, obscurity, the apparatus of modern life ('any kind of experience'), his rhymed octosyllabic stanzas demonstrated how much the age could learn from the Metaphysical poets. From the dramatists of the previous period, particularly the 'decadent' Jacobean dramatists, he learnt how the blank verse line could be made flexible, 'unpoetic', capable of admitting the tones and rhythms of speech. Finally, Eliot invented a form of poem which seemed the answer to the problem of incorporating into poetry the vast scope and disorder of the modern world—a world of scientific understanding of society and personality, of a great war and a great revolution, of divided classes, of irreligion and the need for moral standards. For the poets of the twenties Eliot was, above all, the author of *The Waste Land*, that deliberately inexplicit but enormously significant poem which welded quotations, personal memories, urban experience and a disillusioned tone round an anthropological insight into human culture and a yearning for the good life.

In one sense, however, the method of *The Waste Land* (and of Pound's *Cantos*, which made their way to a public at a later date) was stillborn. It produced several direct imitations and as late as 1929 was still siring undergraduate poetry, but only Ronald Bottrall of the young poets of the late twenties continued to exploit it. It reflected too completely the actual waste land of the twenties—the arid and fevered intellectual landscape which was already hatching 'beliefs' calculated to change completely poetry's tone and aim. So, too, the adoption by a number of poets of the metaphysical style, though enabling them to write some brilliant poetry, only begged the question of the 'belief' underneath the style. In the verse of a characteristic and excellent poet of the twenties, Edgell Rickword, there constantly rises, between the celebrations of unsatisfactory love and the sordid unfriendliness of cities, an obsession with the barrenness of thought—the 'cold, deserted mind', the 'earth-haunted mind that moves obscure among symbolical forests seeking pure immutable forms.'

Eliot's precepts and example drenched the twenties, but there had previously been a blow dealt the old poetic diction and ideas which the twenties had perhaps forgotten. The best poetry of the First World War, particularly that of Wilfred Owen and Siegfried Sassoon, broke sharply away from the poetry of the preceding period. Sassoon, before joining the Army, had been a nature poet in a mild and 'poetic' tradition. In his autobiographies he describes how a realist, laconic, candid, colloquial style was, as it were, forced on him by his growing pacifism and his desire to report the life of the front line. Owen added to realism a deep perception of the duties of the poet in the modern world which he expressed not only in his verse but also in the fragmentary preface to the collection of poems he never lived to publish: 'Above all I am not concerned with Poetry. . . . All a poet can do today is warn. That is why the true Poets must be truthful.' Owen also exploited brilliantly a technical device—the half-rhyme—which, like Eliot's technical discoveries, was designed to avoid the 'poeticism' in which the late Victorians had been bogged down:

> *Sit on the bed. I'm blind, and three parts shell.*
> *Be careful; can't shake hands now; never shall.*

The end of the First World War coincided with the delayed publication of the verse of a remarkable Victorian poet, Gerard Manley Hopkins. Hopkins had freed himself from the enervating rhythmical smoothness of Tennysonian poetry by rediscovering the old English tradition of 'sprung-rhythm' in which the elastic stresses of the verse line, by being as little mechanical as possible and independent of syllable counting, enabled him to put into practice his other great precept—'that the poetical language should be the current language heightened, to any degree heightened and unlike it, but not . . . an obsolete one.'

Lastly, there was the extraordinary metamorphosis of a poet who had already achieved fame at the turn of the century. The poetry of W. B. Yeats had embodied the abstract desire for 'beauty' of the eighteen nineties, quintessentially so because of its remote, dreamlike use of Celtic legend. But with the sharpening during the new century of Ireland's struggle for independence from British rule Yeats' poetry changed. He had desired to help his country in the field of the theatre, and through the drama's need for plain contact with a wide audience he came to realize the need for directness and realism in the style and subjects of his lyric poetry also. Like Sassoon he has recorded in the clearest terms his shedding of the 'poeticism' of the preceding period, as in these words from a letter of 1905: 'I am now correcting the last few lines [of *The Shadowy Waters*], and have joyfully got "creaking shoes" and "liquorice-root" into what had been a very abstract passage. I believe more strongly every day that the element of strength in poetic language is common idiom. . . .'

3

The nineteen thirties were ushered in by a vast economic crisis in the western world, which led to mass unemployment, the strengthening of violent and reactionary political parties and the consequent threat of a second world war. The cultured and hitherto protected sector of society from which poets spring was threatened with the same insecurity and doom as proletarian man: the issues of poetry seemed suddenly to be bound up with the question of the survival of civilized and libertarian society. As has been seen, the poetical terms in which the crisis was to be treated had already been determined. The experimental and neo-metaphysical poets of the twenties had tried to heal the split in sensibility which Eliot had diagnosed: his collected poems were published in 1925 and exerted an immense influence in *avant garde* circles. Yeats brought out in 1928 a splendid volume in his new style, *The Tower*, which contained a meditative sequence on the Irish Civil War—an anticipation, as it were, of a theme that was to engross the succeeding decade. In 1930 the work of Hopkins became widely known for the first time through the enlarged second edition of his poems, and a second impression was called for within six months. Owen enjoyed a similar extension of reputation and influence through the complete edition of his verse which appeared in 1931.

But despite these strong and salutary influences, English poetry in the thirties was largely dominated and directed by the genius of a new poet, W. H. Auden, who from the publication of his first (publicly printed) volume in 1930 exerted the compulsive stylistic force of a Milton, a Wagner, a Picasso. Auden had learnt from Eliot, Hopkins, Owen—but also from the most unlikely (as it seemed then) and diverse elements in poetry: Langland, for example, and Emily Dickinson. He reached out for various styles, various forms, and into them went the phenomena of the time—the moral bankruptcy of the ruling class; the conspiracies of the ruled; deserted docks, rusting machines and crumbling farms; the hopes for a new and socially just society. Allied to his great interest in the diversified types of a modern civilization was a grasp of the discoveries about human personality by Freud, about society by Marx: the result was a power of generalization whose pregnant and brilliant form haunted the minds (and pages) of other poets of the day.

Whatever qualifications and hesitancies there were in Auden and the poets who were associated with his name through the anthologies and periodicals of the period, there is no doubt that in retrospect they must be seen as dissident artists, accepting the conception that modern poetry must often be complex and experimental, yet close to the language of its age must try, in the difficult conditions of a divided culture, to find a wider audience to whom to speak its truths and warnings. Thus they were, like Yeats, led into the theatre: and many of them for several years wore the rebellious public Audenesque mask in denial (as it proved) of their real talents and inclinations.

The 'beliefs' which animated the characteristic verse of the thirties did not survive the bewildering events at the end of the epoch. The Moscow trials, the defeat of Republican Spain, the alleviation of unemployment through the expansion of the armaments industry, the Nazi-Soviet pact; the outbreak of the 'wrong' war —these blurred not only the poets' allegiances but also their aims. Auden himself left for the United States in 1938; even before that his contemporary Stephen Spender had begun to produce verse about which he said: 'I have deliberately turned back to a kind of writing which is more personal, and I have included within my subjects weakness and fantasy and illusion,' while the start of war dealt the death blow to two 'little' magazines, Geoffrey Grigson's *New Verse* and Julian Symons' *Twentieth Century Verse* which had printed the new poetry and maintained severe (and often waspish) editorial standards against all that was phoney, archaic, unclear, sterilely-academic, in modern verse and its criticism.

4

The poetry written by poets serving in the forces during the Second World War on the whole reflected faithfully this confusion and abdication. Confusion: that the instrument which was used against fascist Germany was an England which, whatever its spirit and allies, had not changed its social structure, made such poets cynical and doubtful of all but private values. For them there could be no whole-hearted return to the indignation at war, the simple assertion of civilized human rights, expressed by Owen and Sassoon. Alun Lewis, one of the best of them, summed up the dilemma acutely: 'Acceptance seems so spiritless, protest so vain. In between the two I live.' Abdication: almost all the best poets who were under 35 in 1939 never served in the armed forces at all and so missed the impact of the universal experience of those years.

All the same, an important part of the ideals and achievements of thirties poetry survived through the war years. A number of service poets, though their poems tend to peter out in self-pity and a mere assertion of the value of personal love, gave clear and sometimes moving pictures of their life. Alun Lewis himself began in his last poems to express a deeper conception of the crisis of Western civilization: his *The Jungle Pool* has, like Owen's *Strange Meeting* the profound and measured pessimism that could have been the herald of a new synthesis of belief. And Keith Douglas, who was born as late as 1920, still used an intellectual approach to poetry and was most successful in giving his verse the fresh ring of speech: he was, too, ironical rather than self-pitiful about his situation. (The death on active service of both Lewis and Douglas was a great loss: their sanity and intelligence would have stiffened the crumbling front of post-war poetry.) The platform and encouragement for this extension of the thirties spirit of accurate reporting and clarity of vision was the remarkable continuance of John Lehmann's *New Writing* in its hard-cover and Penguin forms.

Strangely enough (though possibly not very strangely) it was the work of a woman poet, Edith Sitwell, that the impact of the war perhaps most changed and deepened: after 1939 it showed a new concern for the fate of common humanity—acquired, in fact, a wider 'belief' in its purpose.

5

An opposition to the Auden-inspired poets and editors was perceptible from the middle thirties. It is important to distinguish between the nature of the initial opposition and that to which it later declined. The first inklings that a non-rational poetry was possible in the Auden era came perhaps at the time of the late arrival of surrealism to these shores, imported in its literary form through the original poetry, translations and exposition of a young writer called David Gascoyne. Gascoyne's early poems proceeded through the addition of image after outrageous image in a free verse form: he had no interest in the techniques that had been opened up through the rediscovery of Hopkins and Auden's own resuscitation of classical forms (which, incidentally, included such ostensibly artificial vehicles as Locksley Hall metre and the sestina). There is no doubt that the sanction of surrealist practice inspired the early poetry of Dylan

Thomas, but in his case the moving body of images was conveyed by rhymed verse and resounding iambic lines:

> *Murmur of spring nor crush the cockerel's eggs,*
> *Nor hammer back a season in the figs. . . .*

The same freedom of imagery, the shift of emphasis to the poet's interior concerns, a slackening of the puritanical effort to be understood, to warn, to moralize, was also seen in the work of another promising poet of the later thirties, George Barker. But, of course, surrealism had left-wing political attachments, and at first neither Thomas nor Barker differed essentially in their ideological allegiances from the prevailing temper of thirties poets. Both, in fact, contributed to the organs of the new poetry.

In the event, however, the purely poetic in their work provided the inspiration for the growth of a body of verse for verse's sake. The Thomas manner was often a mere veneer over an essential poeticism: thus in a book by one of the epigoni published in 1945 we find on one page: 'Swung from the ropes of his father's cackled rhyme,' and on another:

> *There is no sweeter sight, I swear, in Heaven*
> *Than blossom on the cherry-trees by Clee.*

As the thirties closed there was an accession of power to eclectic periodicals and critics. The plausible doctrines flourished of judging a poem by its 'beauty', of crying anathema to groups and cliques, of proclaiming the independence of poetry from external pressures. When the rump of the thirties dissolved with the end of the war, a sad decline of standards was found among young poets. Because the *raison d'être* of poetry had weakened, technical skill had lessened. Since 1945 only during the last two or three years has there been evidence of appropriate poetic aims in the work of new poets.

6

F. R. Leavis in the 1950 edition of his *New Bearings in English Poetry*, pointed out Eliot's extraordinary change in a few years from disreputable *avant garde* poet to respected man of letters. This change was, of course, in the eyes of the don and of what an American critic has expressively characterized as 'the cultivated middle-brow zombie'. But the process was certainly accelerated by Eliot's own development. While his earlier poetry was fathering the movement of the thirties, he himself was incubating a reaction. His verse, from *Ash Wednesday* (1930), solved the problem of 'belief' by becoming openly Christian. In the later series of poems collected in 1944 under the title *Four Quartets*, the Christian ideas are so essential that some critics (and no doubt readers) have passed off exegesis as literary criticism. These ideas and this attitude have, after the failure of the radical beliefs of the thirties, helped to make Eliot's later verse widely acceptable. And with that has come the critical if not the practical acceptance of his parallel suspicion of figurative language, of words themselves, of his assertion that the poet's highest task is to make poetry that can be looked through, not *at*—'to get *beyond poetry*', as he said in 1935, 'as Beethoven, in his later works, strove to get beyond music.'

And yet the strongest parts of the *Quartets*, it seems to me, are those which use imagery and observation in the old Eliotesque way (and this is what accounts for the superiority of *The Dry Salvages* over the other three poems):

> *The pointed scrutiny with which we challenge*
> *The first-met stranger in the waning dusk. . . .*

and those passages of verbal and ironic virtuosity of the kind that marked his earlier verse—that, for example, beginning 'To communicate with Mars, converse with spirits. . . .'

Conversely what is most unlikely to wear well is the vague and generalized symbolism—the rose, the Chinese jar, the garden (cf. the conversation about gardens, dangerously near banality, in Act II of *The Confidential Clerk*). One is reminded of Wyndham Lewis's remark about Pound's early influence on Eliot, that the latter 'was lifted out of his lunar alley-ways and *fin de siècle* nocturnes, into a massive region of verbal creation in contact with that astonishing didactic intelligence,' and one wonders if those parts of the *Quartets* are not a kind of recidivism. Eliot's Beethoven parallel, in fact, requires severe qualification: in Beethoven's last work it is not the abandonment of the gross means of music— melody, imitation, exploitation of the instrument—but their extraordinarily pure, studied and accurate use which makes for greatness.

Arnold Bennett in his *Journal* recounts a meeting with Eliot in 1924 when the poet said that he 'wanted to write a drama of modern life (furnished flat sort of people) in a rhythmic prose "perhaps with certain things in it accentuated by drum-beats."' It would be interesting to know whether that remarkable prefiguration of the later plays included so much of the conventional frame- work, characterisation, ideas, as they actually possess and which has helped to secure for them a popular success. *The Cocktail Party* and *The Confidential Clerk* show a fine effort to produce a workable theatrical form in a language above the level of the 'serious' West End play, but one misses those drum-beats!

> *If we're having two wines with a meal, then I serve*
> *either a glass of champagne beforehand, or a very dry*
>   *sherry.*
> *I don't think it's a good thing to be stunned*
> *with alcohol before a meal—or at any time, come to that.*

Of course, that is not Eliot: it comes from an article in the smart magazine *House and Garden* where it was so typographically arranged. But it shows the dangers inherent in the verse and milieu of Eliot's later drama.

Because of Eliot's development he is felt to be a different kind of poet from those who ruled the twenties and thirties: his verse before *Ash Wednesday* has loosened its hold on the young and is perhaps undervalued. So, too, Auden's United States citizenship has changed the nature of his influence: in America he has found the conditions and inspiration for the writing of long poems whose very fertility and technical experimentation have militated against their whole-hearted acceptance in the markedly different conditions which have prevailed on this side of the Atlantic: while freed from his orbit those poets who were associated with his name in the thirties have gone their individual paths.

Of such poets the most steadfast and the most responsive to the demands of the changing age has proved to be Spender. His introspection towards the end of the thirties could not withstand the tragedies of the early part of the war: his *Ruins and Visions* of 1942 embodied, in a masterly way, our deepest feelings about the shattering European events. No other public themes have since inspired him and though his verse has never ceased to probe and experiment—moving from the eloquent and marmoreal free line of his first book through a period of rhymed verse back to a barer and shorter line—his most fruitful work since the war has been critical. He grasped very early the central problem of the ambitious poet in a society opposed to poetry—how (as he has recently written) 'to be able to relate his talents to the life of his times, so that through them he can transform a wide experience of the life of that time into his poetry'; how to 'transmute the anti-poetic material of modern life into transparent poetry'; how to find a belief which will 'put man at the centre of his poetry'.

These have been the dominant themes of all Spender's critical writing from *The Destructive Element* (1935) to *The Making of a Poem* (1955). It is easy no doubt to attack his insistence on 'belief' and his refusal really to specify it or the precise way in which one can put 'the creative imagination back at the centre of life'; all this certainly looks too much like a yearning for socialism without facing up to its distasteful ways and means. But Spender's dogged concern with these essential considerations has preserved him from the 'poetry for poetry's sake' or the purely literary by-ways which have ossified or narrowed the attitude and therefore the work of some of his contemporaries.

Of the two other poets whose names were coupled with Auden and Spender's in the revival of the thirties, Cecil Day Lewis has left behind, perhaps with relief, the cares of social engagement and of thirties diction, and emerged as a poet often deliberately 'poetical' who, despite his elaborate craftsmanship and varied output, has really ceased to contribute to the issues which this essay has tried to uncover. Louis MacNeice has developed in a different way. His concern to bear the burden of the times arose late in the thirties when he was already distinguished as a poet of high spirits, telling observation, bull's-eye image, writing in the easy tones which Auden had established but a little aside from the main Audenesque stream. Since the break-up of the thirties movement he has made strenuous efforts to establish a philosophic standpoint from which to treat the themes of the modern situation. Just how much was lost with the decay of radicalism can be seen in the group of poems called 'The Kingdom' which MacNeice published in *Springboard* (1944). It begins:

> *Under the surface of flux and of fear there is an underground movement,*
> *Under the crust of bureaucracy, quiet behind the posters,*
> *Unconscious but palpably there—the kingdom of individuals.*

Later the members of the Kingdom are characterized:

> *Take this old man with the soldierly straight back*
> *Dressed in tweeds like a squire but he has not a squire's presumption,*
> *His hands are gentle with wild flowers, his memory*
> *Latticed with dialect and anecdotes*
> *And wisps of nature poetry; he is of the kingdom,*
> *A country-lover and very English, the cadence*
> *Of Christmas bells in his voice. . . . .*

The degeneration in ideas and language is surprising: 'soldierly', 'tweeds', 'very English', 'cadence of Christmas bells'—these are conceptions which in the thirties would only have been the subject of satire. I underline what I think to be a failure of conception and hence of diction here because it illustrates my thesis so well, but it is ungenerous to MacNeice whose post-thirties work has elsewhere—particularly in *Ten Burnt Offerings* (1952)—been far more successful in enlarging its subject matter and verse forms.

It is a younger poet, Lawrence Durrell, who of the Auden group (the phrase is used imprecisely) has, it seems to me, most successfully come through the post-war years. His more ambitious pieces, because of the lack of a morality, of an attitude towards experience, have sometimes a dilettante air, but his intelligence and wit, his fastidious use of words, and precise evocation of a scene (usually the Mediterranean), have enabled him to write many distinguished if marginal poems. Other poets of Durrell's generation have avoided the difficulties of the Auden line by assuming a Bardic role, with Yeats or Dylan Thomas at the back of their minds.

On the whole the direct influence of Yeats is an impossible one. His plainer manner—the flexible but unfaltering iambic line, the unemphatic rhymes which nevertheless clinch the thought—is fingerprinted with the myth of the private life he made public:

> *John Synge, I and Augusta Gregory, thought*
> *All that we did, all that we said or sang*
> *Must come from contact with the soil, from that*
> *Contact everything Anteaus-like grew strong.*

His more rhapsodic manner, associated with his consummate use of the three beat line, is still more personal to him. Even Vernon Watkins, a skilful and dedicated poet, has failed to transform the Yeatsian idiom into a vehicle for fresh departures.

It was the more obscure and clotted of Dylan Thomas's first poems which prompted that direct imitation I have already mentioned, but the influence was too constricting to make the group of imitators anything more than a temporary curiosity. Thomas himself, in the long interval between *Deaths and Entrances* (1946) and his previous collection, extended his interests, clarified his diction and elaborated his forms. Even in such a poet the result of the break-up of the thirties ideals and critical standards can be seen. His direct experience of the war was confined to the air-raids on London: these and his lost youth (though in 1946 he was only 32) formed the main themes of his later poetry, themes often decorated with rhetoric, typographical shapes, double substantives, and breaking sometimes (as in a poem like *Fern Hill*) into a sentimentality that perhaps helps to account for the extraordinary popularity he gained after his death.

7

The last twenty-five years have seen a number of individual and rather isolated poets who have developed their talents away from the line of what may be called 'legislative' poetry, but yet have understood and practised the century's poetic rehabilitation. Of these the most important is Robert Graves, who, indeed, both alone and with Laura Riding, helped in the rehabilitation and was a not inconsiderable influence on Auden. Through his soldiering in the First World War, his early knowledge of poets of the American Renaissance like Ransom, his sharp nose for inflated feeling and language, his insight into personal relationships, his appreciation of his own limits and powers, Graves has produced a body of verse of consistently high standard—elegant, ironic, formidably intelligent. A feature of the Gravesian poem is often a myth created for the purpose of the poem:

> *Beyond the Atlas roams a love-beast;*
> *The aborigines harry it with darts. . . .*

Or:

> *By sloth on sorrow fathered,*
> *These dusty-featured Lollocks*
> *Have their nativity in all disordered*
> *Backs of cupboard drawers. . . .*

An otherwise very dissimilar poet, Edwin Muir, has also written poems of that scheme, the myth often abstracted from the obsessive elements of modern European life—a frontier, a fight to the death between two unequal combatants. And in the poetry of one younger than these (who emerged, in fact, with the Auden school), William Empson, myth appears in the form of Donne-like images, worked out with metaphysical tightness:

> *All those large dreams by which men long live well*
> *Are magic-lanterned on the smoke of hell;*
> *This then is real, I have implied,*
> *A painted, small, transparent slide.*

The methods of Graves, Muir and Empson enable their poetry to make a moral comment undetermined, as it were, by considerations outside the individual poem. Some of the most promising of the young poets who have arisen since the war, lacking 'belief', have seized upon this *modus operandi*. Thom Gunn, for example, has written poems of the potted imaginary history type:

> *Bandit to prince was his advance one night,*
> *He soon was overthrown, he was exiled. . . .*

94

D. J. Enright, though his stimulus is usually his visual sense, often relies on the tough, ironic, Gravesian tone to round off his observations, as in his excellent poem on the Demon of the Japanese Noh plays:

> *Terrible enough, this demon. Yet it is present and perfect,*
> *Firm as its horns, curling among its thick and handsome*
>   *hair.*
> *I find it an honest visitant, even consoling, after all*
> *These sententious phantoms, choked with rage and uncer-*
>   *tainty,*
> *Who grimace from contemporary pages. . . .*

Some of the youngest poets have gone to the even more constricted and strongly-marked manner of Empson and have been adversely criticized for so doing. But it is a natural and on the whole healthy reaction against the sloppy technique and absence of thought of the poetic post-war years. It does not however solve the central problem of the young poet writing to-day; a neo-Empsonian who is also a true poet will not long be content with the prim and barren moral apothegm that frequently comes out of the end of a poem in the manner of the Master. And too often the tight seventeenth-century style shades off into the pat eighteenth-century style.

Nor, however much one admires Graves, can one believe that the isolated position he has found or been forced into and which for him has been so stimulating, is the right one for poets with a different history or talent. He has said: 'To write poems for other than poets is wasteful.' The poet is our society may well at times be doomed to a public of poets, but it seems to me to be death to poetry to write only with such a public in mind.

8

The recognition by the newest poets of the dilemma of 'neutralism', their interest in strict verse forms and ratiocinative poems, gives one more optimism about the future of poetry than there has been grounds for during the whole of the last decade. There is about the situation a faint whiff of the twenties, but what is lacking is the twenties experimentalism. History, as Marx said, cannot repeat itself except as farce, and there is something ridiculous (and disturbing) about the disillusion (and the illusions) of some of the young intellectuals which can be seen most clearly in the novels of John Wain and Kingsley Amis (who are also good poets). Talented and amusing though these fictions are, they attack society and culture from a vaguely revolutionary and fundamentally sentimental standpoint that in the thirties we would have been testing for signs of an incipient fascism. They are often, simply, not 'true'. If a way out of the compulsion of the short poem is to be found, if people and narrative are to be brought back to poetry, if there is to be a secular poetic drama, poets must find an attitude, a belief, that will enable them to be truthful.

The problem is also, as I have tried to show, one of style, of diction. The line—the example, rather—of Hopkins, Pound, Eliot, Owen, Auden; of common speech heightened, of a poetry of 'belief', of social value, has been blurred by recent anthologies, eclectic verse magazines, by the development of poets and critics of the Auden generation, and it is not easy to see how it may be continued. (Auden himself, by ransacking the past of his art—as Picasso and Stravinsky ransacked theirs—so brilliantly and so completely for his own purposes has added to the difficulty. Perhaps for young poets one way round this immense father figure—who seems to some to have already said everything worth saying about the contemporary situation—is by a return to realism, as for painters I suppose that is one way round Picasso.) But anyway, poetry is overdue for one of its periodical cleansings of all that is 'poetical'.

In the last analysis the development of any art depends on social and political influences. On the short term view prolonged economic crisis or a substantial lessening of tension between East and West would possibly induce in poetry a sprouting of those seeds of change which at present are barely detectable. Certainly, poetry since the war has been dominated by the peculiar mental nihilism and *laisser faire* which has arisen from the combination of freedom from want and the threat of atomic destruction.

On the longer—and necessarily vaguer—view the poet, like every artist in our society, ignored by mass culture, will always be tempted (if only unconsciously) to throw in his lot with 'middlebrow' culture, the culture of false seriousness, dead tradition and compromise. His problem is to remain a part of minority culture and yet find a way for society, if it wills, to discover at any time in his work the expression of those values on which its future depends.

The Poet and His Medium

G. S. FRASER

M̲R ROY FULLER, in another essay in this volume,
has given a critical sketch of the development of
English poetry over the past twenty-five years.
My subject, though I cover the same field and period, is
a humbler one. The poet's medium, in the primary and
most important application of the phrase, is language;
but language communicates, and you and I, in so far as
he works upon us, and we work upon him, are part of his
medium, too. It is with certain secondary applications of
the word 'medium' that I am here most directly concerned, those that have a special bearing on the relation
between the poet and his audience and therefore, more
remotely, on the place and prestige of the poet in the
wider literary world.

In my secondary range of applications, the poet's media
would, for instance, at a trivial level include even his
pen or his typewriter (and which he chooses of these can,
in fact, make a considerable difference to his methods of
composition); they would include also the friends to
whom he may read early drafts of poems, sometimes
correcting these according to their advice; the literary
groups among which he moves, being affected by their
standards; the public platform which may enable him

to test the effect of his poems on a larger audience; the anthologies and periodicals in which he is able to compare his work with that of his contemporaries; the pamphlet or volume solely devoted to his work, which may first draw the attention of reviewers to him; the radio microphone; the gramophone record; and, if the poet is a verse dramatist, or can use verse for documentary purposes, the stage, the television screen, the cinema screen. Many of these media are very new. Some of them have yet been very little exploited by poets. Television producers do not yet quite know what to do with poetry. My friend, the poet and critic, Geoffrey Moore, had a six months' course training as a television producer, in which he was concerned precisely with this problem. The only bright idea I could think of, to suggest to him, was a programme of Chinese poems in versions by Mr. Waley and Mr. Pound accompanied by pictures of Chinese paintings. Dr. I. A. Richards, on one of his regrettably infrequent visits to England, made the brilliantly simple suggestion that the reading aloud of the poem should be accompanied by a visual projection of the words being read. But that problem is not solved; and if we think of poetry in the cinema, though Cocteau has made a brilliant use of poetic *ideas*, the only notable uses of modern *verse* one can think of are the film of *Murder in the Cathedral* and Mr. Auden's verse accompaniment, in the 1930s, to *Night Mail*.

As regards sound radio, the case is very different: it could be plausibly argued that in recent years the Third Programme has done much more to put new poets across to a wide audience than either publishers or editors of periodicals. The circulation of small magazines devoted solely to verse rarely tops three thousand and more often

BELMONT COLLEGE LIBRARY

ranges around one thousand; and they can seldom afford to pay their contributors. A first impression of a first volume of verse rarely consists of more than a thousand and sometimes of as few as five hundred copies; the usual advance on royalties on it is between ten and twenty pounds. Very few poets, indeed, ever seriously hope to make a living out of their poems. Still, a fairly long poem, like Mr. W. S. Graham's *The Night Fishing*, that may take forty minutes or so to broadcast, will net its author about a pound a minute when it is first produced, and about two thirds of that sum when it is repeated; and it will reach an audience of many thousands of people, a much wider audience than regularly buy either poetry periodicals or new volumes of verse. A remarkable young American poet, Mr. W. S. Merwin, who has been living in this country for some years, is reputed to have earned a reasonably comfortable living largely from original poems and verse translations commissioned for broadcasting. Thus, for the poet as for other imaginative writers, the printed page is beginning to lose its old central authority. The word as seen has now to compete with the word as heard; it may soon have to compete with the heard word as an accompaniment to visual action.

It is possible to take—as, for instance, Mr. J. B. Priestley takes—a somewhat gloomy view of the effect of the new 'mass media' on imaginative writing. Mr. Priestley's view, roughly, is that the imaginative writer 'working in' with film or television or radio producers soon finds that he is a subordinate and relatively badly paid member of a large team of technicians; and that he must subordinate his vision, also, to the technicians' idea of what the medium can 'carry' and what the audience will 'take.'

For poets, at least, there is a more cheerful side to the picture. In the B.B.C., as I say, they have found a new patron and a new audience which, though large, is not impersonal; for one of the most elementary rules of broadcasting technique is that (Mr. Louis MacNeice has made the point, in passing, in a long poem) though one is addressing an enormous number of individuals, one is addressing each one of them individually; the rhetoric of the microphone, even if it has its own intrinsic dangers, is as far as possible from the rhetoric of the platform, the rhetoric which fires or subdues the crowd. The microphone also enables the poet to get past certain barriers which, for the ordinary reader of poetry on the page, remain uncomfortably real. The uninstructed lover of poetry, who listens in regularly to verse programmes, soon learns to trust his ear as well as his eye; he learns that he possesses a natural sense of rhythm; he gives up the bad habit of counting stresses and syllables on his fingers. Listening to a poet reading his own work can, also, be in some ways a more intimate experience than getting a first impression of his work from the printed page. The imagined timbre of a poet's voice is a very important element, indeed, in the appreciation of much great poetry (thus, Saintsbury talks about the 'sad clangour' of Donne's voice and Dr. Richards calls Donne 'one of the slowest movers in all English poetry'). Not all poets are effective readers of their own work, in not every case does the outer voice convey the timbre of the inner voice; but Mr. T. S. Eliot, for instance, and Mr. William Empson are two difficult poets whose broadcastings of their own work—with its extremely individual rhythms, pauses, overtones, and emphases—must have deepened many a listener's understanding and enjoyment. (It must also have forced upon some listeners, new to that work, that immediate emotional apprehension of a difficult poem that can safely precede intellectual comprehension of it, by a long period in time.)

We have been dealing with the educative effect of a new medium on the audience; but any new medium also, of course, educates those who use it. Radio, as a new technique, has had to produce its own new forms; and these forms, when handled by a poet, can acquire an intrinsic literary value. Radio verse plays like Mr. Louis MacNeice's *The Dark Tower* or Mr. Laurie Lee's *Magellan* could not have been conceived, for instance, either as actable stage plays or as 'closet dramas': the microphone was their midwife. Dylan Thomas's *Under Milk Wood*, a minor comic masterpiece, is conceived entirely in terms of radio; it is a fantastication of that familiar radio form, the sentimental, descriptive, semi-dramatised 'feature' about a small place; it has no strictly 'literary' ancestors. And, at a less radically experimental level, long poems or sequences of poems like Mr. Louis MacNeice's *Ten Burnt Offerings* or Mr. Cecil Day Lewis's *An Italian Visit* have obviously been composed both with the potentialities and the limitations of the sound medium in mind. They are reflective, discursive, tangential poems, that both in their largeness and looseness recall the conversational poetry of the Victorian age, recall Browning or Clough, say. They represent a break-away from the idea of the tight, short poem as the 'standard' poem, and whether or not one approves of that break-away, it is radio that has made it possible (the ear is in some ways more patient than the eye).

Finally, we should note that over the last few years many poets of a younger generation than those I have been mentioning have made their first impact on a wide audience through programmes like Mr. Lehmann's 'New Soundings', Mr. John Wain's 'First Reading', my own and later Mr. Iain Fletcher's 'New Poetry' (selections of poems from current periodicals and books), and 'New Verse', a series of programmes of unpublished work, selected on each occasion by a different poet. I often wonder whether what one might call 'radio-consciousness' has something to do with the current fashion among a whole group of younger poets—poets like Mr. Thom Gunn, Mr. Philip Larkin, Mr. John Wain, Mr. Donald Davie, and at least half a dozen others—for a very plain, crisp style and for combination of extreme metrical regularity with a conversational order of words. It may have, though other young poets, like Mr. Christopher Logue or Mr. Richard Murphy, who do not all admire this 'neo-Augustan' mode have also written poems admirably suited to broadcasting. There is, on the other hand, a kind of poem which may be a good poem, and to which the microphone cannot always do justice, the logically or syntactically intricate poem like some of Donne's or some of Mr. Empson's, or, among young writers, like most of Mr. Alfred Alvarez's poems. If the ear is more intelligent than the eye about rhythms and emphases, the eye is more intelligent than the ear about the kind of connexions that work both back and forwards in a poem. (Ideally when we can we should listen with the text that is being broadcast in front of us.) But it is not this kind of intricacy that is usually either the forte or the foible of young poets; and the microphone does help most young poets very much by showing up mercilessly faked rhythms, loose grammar, muddled sentiments, and tones pitched too high.

2

Radio offers us, then, the most obviously fruitful field for a study of the effect of one of the poet's secondary media on his primary medium, language. But his more traditional secondary medium, the printed page, should certainly not be ignored. Over the last twenty-five years, I have noted three distinct phases in the fashions in which young poets of promise first burst into print. Between about 1930 and about 1940, the new poet of promise might, after acquiring a reputation at his university and perhaps publishing a slim pamphlet there, make his first appearance before a wider world in some 'group' anthology, announcing a new trend, like the famous *New Signatures*. His first important volume would then be published by some large and well-established firm, with a high reputation by no means merely centred on poetry, of the type of Faber, Chatto and Windus, or Jonathan Cape. In the 1940s, publishers like the Hogarth Press or Routledge were still eager to give a start to poets of the quality of Mr. Terence Tiller, Mr. Laurie Lee, or Mr. Norman McCaig. A big firm like Faber at once pounced on Mr. Lawrence Durrell. And because every large war always produces a fine mixed crop of new poets and new would-be poets many well-established publishers brought out anthologies of wartime verse, anthologies which were always uneven but which introduced such poets as, for instance, Alun Lewis, Sidney Keyes, and Keith Douglas to a wide public. Editors of literary periodicals with a wide circulation, like Mr. John Lehmann in *Penguin New Writing*—and to a lesser degree Mr. Cyril Connolly in *Horizon*, for his touch with poetry had never been very sure—extended a discrimina-

ting welcome to some of the best of the newer names.
Yet on the whole the average young poet of the 1940s did
not feel that the older publishers or the more famous
periodicals were his likeliest market. Between about 1940
and 1950, he would more typically make his first appearance in periodicals of the type of *Poetry Quarterly* or *Poetry
London* or perhaps in one of a number of 'new romantic'
anthologies; his first volume was less likely to be brought
out by a large publisher than by the Grey Walls Press
or Poetry London (the firms which ran the two periodicals
mentioned), fairly small and in the end fairly short-lived
concerns, mainly interested in the publishing of poetry.

Since about 1950, many of the most promising of the
newer poets have come out first in more modest format,
with still smaller publishers: in the ninepenny pamphlets
and paper-backed volumes of the Fantasy Press at Oxford,
in the advance-subscribed soft-covered volumes printed,
under the editorship of Mr. John Wain, by the School of
Art at the University of Reading, or in the pamphlets
and paper-backed small volumes published by Miss Erica
Marx's Hand and Flower Press. There are cheering signs,
as I write, that the larger publishers are once again
becoming interested in new poetry, but on the whole
over our period the publishing of poetry has tended to
become a growingly specialist (and perhaps a growingly
altruistic) activity.

The specialization has also extended to the audience.
Mr. Auden's poems, in the 1930s, appealed to anyone
who was interested in literature or, indeed, sensitively
interested in public affairs. In the 1940s, following up
new poets had become almost a specialized activity, like
bird-watching; one had a feeling also that the 'little
magazines' of verse were read largely by people wanting

to write for them; and that there was a cleavage between a bohemian, Soho-centred 'poetry 'world' and a wider and smarter 'literary world' which rather looked askance at it. The poets of the 1950s may often have an equally small audience, but it is a different one. Both the Fantasy Press and the University of Reading School of Art Press function in a university world. Most of the Fantasy pamphlets are by undergraduates; many of the new poets who have taken their degrees are university teachers. The poet has typically functioned, one may say, in three successive generations in 'the great world', the bohemian world, and the academic world. And, similarly, typical new poets of the generations of the 1930s, the 1940s, and the 1950s have differed widely in their choice of theme, their basic moral attitudes to life, their feeling about language, about the audience. I once had the pleasure, in the Caves de France in Soho, of introducing a poet of the 1950s, Mr. Donald Davie, who teaches English in Dublin, to Mr. Wrey Gardiner, who edited *Poetry Quarterly* and helped to run the Grey Walls Press in the 1940s, and to Mr. Randall Swingler, who has vivid memories of the political excitements of the 1930s. It was an amiable occasion, but one was aware, at the same time, very vividly, of the invisible roadblocks that hampered any real communication. Not only the poet as a type, but the concept of poetry, suffers change.

Does this narrowing and specializing of the audience for, at least, printed poetry mean that, since around 1940, poetry, by new poets, has been getting steadily worse: or, on the other hand, that the tastes of the reading public have been getting steadily coarser? I would be reluctant to accept, without qualification, either conclusion.

Anything one says about public taste must be a guess, largely. But when I look at things like the growing success of Pelican Books, for instance, or the huge and mixed audience which crowded the Royal Festival Hall for the Coronation poetry reading and the Dylan Thomas memorial reading—and when I think, too, of my personal experiences at week-end residential Adult Education colleges—I am inclined to think that there is a much larger stratum of the British people than there used to be that is genuinely eager to get in touch with 'the best that has been thought and said'; one should not allow oneself to be excessively depressed by Fleet Street's commercial exploitation of crime and sex, or by stories about Teddy Boys. There is a steady, and steadying, element in the nation that could respond to poetry.

Nor when I think of some of the poets who have come into notice since 1940—poets so different, so variously gifted, as Mr. David Gascoyne, Mr. W. S. Graham, Mr. Lawrence Durrell, Mr. Laurie Lee, Mr. Thom Gunn—do I think that there has been a decline in the average level of poetic talent, even though it is true that, since about 1940, no new poets have emerged with the dominating prestige of Mr. Eliot, or Mr. Auden, or even Dylan Thomas. We may be going through a period of minor poetry, but that is not to say that we are going through a period of bad poetry. The real causes for the growing narrowing and specializing of the audience are to be sought elsewhere. I seek them, at least partly, in the different degree to which poets of different generations have been sustained by a sense of social assurance; and also (which is perhaps just saying the same thing in two other ways) in the different degrees of emotional maturity of different generations of poets and the different degrees with which they have been able to tackle public themes, or themes, at least, that have an interest transcending the individual's problems and the problems of his group. What the large public quite rightly demands from poetry is a certain universality, not of reference, but of relevance. There is poetry which in its way may be good poetry, but which does not give them this.

3

The point about the sense of social assurance I can perhaps illustrate by an anecdote. Not very long ago, I had to take the chair for Mr. T. R. H. Henn of Cambridge, when he was talking about Yeats. Mr. Henn himself comes from that almost vanished Irish 'big house' society which so fascinated Yeats, though the poet himself belonged to it only, as it were, by having been co-opted into it. He has personal memories of the 'troubles', which enable him to throw fascinating sidelights on a great poem like *Nineteen Hundred and Nineteen*. He understands intimately the irony of Yeat's relationship to Irish politics—that the triumph of the movement for Southern Irish independence finally destroyed the possibility of that liberal and aristocratic culture which Yeats desired for Ireland. There was an interval, after which Mr. Henn, who can reproduce the very accents of Yeats without parodying them, was going to read aloud some of the greater poems. The first part of the evening had, I thought, been a triumph for Mr. Henn (and for Yeats). But at the bar, in the interval, I saw two young poets whom I knew to be connected with Cambridge, but disciples of a very different Cambridge teacher, Dr. Leavis. The expressions on their faces were extraordinarily sour and resentful. '*We*,' one of them was saying loudly, 'have no "values" and no "manners". Let us sit the next half out.' One could see that they felt themselves in a Dostoevskian sense 'insulted and injured' by Mr. Henn's lecture. I knew both young men, one was almost my friend; but for a moment, I felt that they had indeed no values and no manners . . . without any of these implied inverted commas, which Cambridge intellectuals indicate either by a gesture with the hands or a sudden harsh change in the pitch of the voice.

Has the typical new poet of the last twenty-five years, then, successively, over intervals of five to ten years, lost a little more inner assurance, a little more of a grip on 'values' and 'manners'? Or is the demand that he should have 'values' and 'manners' a false one for us to make of him (what about Rimbaud?)? The bohemian world, which was the typical poetic world of the 1940s, has its own kind of values and manners, its own kind of bitter assurance: which comes out, for instance, in this fine stanza of Mr. George Barker's:

> *Now I know what was wanting in my youth,*
> *It was not water or a loving mouth.*
> *It was what makes the apple-tree grow big,*
> *The mountain fall, and the minnow die.*
> *It was hard cash I needed at my root.*
> *I know now that how I grew was due*
> *To echoing guts and the empty bag—*
> *My song was out of tune for a few notes. . . .*

But bohemianism may not be a matter of objective social conditioning. It may be a matter of choice. The leading poets of the early 1930s went to public schools, and then to Oxford or Cambridge. Dylan Thomas, on

the other hand, went to Swansea Grammar School. His
father was a schoolmaster, and would have liked him to
go to Oxford. Thomas preferred to come to London, to
take all the risks and all the advantages of insecurity and
independence, to establish and exploit his early fame.
His great theme, at the start, would obviously be the
inner turbulence of the adolescent self. Many poets
imitated him, few successfully, in the 1940s: and the
vanishing of the public theme from poetry by young
people in that decade might be related to a remark of
Aristotle's: that very young people cannot discuss politics
or morals intelligently since their lives are a series of
unrelated emotional experiences.

What we have seen, on the other hand, since 1950 is
a new generation of poets, many of them from the equivalent of Swansea Grammar School, but who have won
scholarships to Oxford or Cambridge, and often established themselves as university teachers of English. They
have not the 'political consciousness' of the poets of the
1930s, but, unlike the bohemians of the 1940s, they have
a new kind of prickly 'class consciousness'. Their
assurance tends to be a donnish kind of assurance rather
than broadly human. The best of them, perhaps, feel
sometimes that their academic specialization does harden
their tone and narrow their range. Mr. Donald Davie, I
think, expresses feelings like this in these two elo-
quently harsh stanzas about Cambridge:

> *I wonder still which of the hemispheres*
> *Infects the other, in this grassy globe;*
> *The chumbling moth of Madingley, that blears*
> *The labourer's lamp, destroys the scarlet robe.*

It was the Muse that could not make her home
In that too thin and yet too sluggish air,
Too volatile to live among the loam,
Her sheaves too heavy for the talkers there.

3

Thus, over our period among the new arrivals one gets what one might call three successive social colourings among young poets—smart, bohemian, respectable. (This, of course, is simplified and schematic; it does not apply to war poets like Alun Lewis or Keith Douglas, or, with any useful precision, to a group of exiled civilian poets like Lawrence Durrell, Terence Tiller, and Bernard Spencer, and their Cairo wartime magazine, *Personal Landscape*. Discussing poetry in terms of changing fashions, one finds that one is neglecting talent that was out of step, and attending to non-talent that was in step. Yet a schematic approach, if one bears in mind that it is schematic, may, for the critic, have its secondary uses.) One gets also three main areas of poetic interest: the public world and its problems and the responsibilities of the younger sons of the ruling classes (Auden and his disciples): the turbulence of the inner self seen as reflecting natural turbulence, and a groping through that turbulence for the inner vision (Dylan Thomas and his imitators); and the ironical attitude, both as a technique for emotional self-control and as an aid to social poise in a world recognized as more or less permanently uncomfortable and unsatisfactory (the Amis-Wain-Davie generation). One can also notice that of the two main tendencies in poetic diction over this period, the 'strict' tendency is associated with an upper-middle-class or at least an

academic background, with a sense of political responsibility or at least with an acute awareness, a critical one,
of the social situation; and the 'romantic' tendency is
associated with a lower-middle-class or non-academic
background or at least with a preference for the freedom
of bohemian drift to the haven of administrative securi-
ties. One cannot, much as one would like to keep class-
alignments quite out of the discussion. But in England,
these are infinitely complex.

These different class-alignments express themselves
not only in two different attitudes towards poetry (so
that Dylan Thomas, in the old Nietzschean dichotomy,
is a Dionysian poet and W. H. Auden an Apollonian
one). They also express themselves in the difference of
the social opportunities lying in the way of poets from
one or another of Great Britain's 'two nations'. Poets
like Mr. Louis MacNeice or Mr. Bernard Spencer have
had a training which enables them to take with ease and
confidence to running institutes abroad for the British
Council or planning programmes for the B.B.C. The
danger, indeed, that confronts such poets is that the use
made by society of their administrative aptitudes may
exhaust their poetic energy. A poet, on the other hand,
like Mr. W. S. Graham or Mr. Tom Scott, who, following
his father's footsteps, might have become a fisherman or a
stonemason, is hard to find a niche for; his talent has, in
a sense, exiled him from the working classes (though his
early memories may provide him with the most powerful
images in his poems); but it has not qualified him for the
professional classes. It has qualified him merely as a poet.
And the English social system, with its elaborate system
of in-groups and out-groups, its complicated pecking-
order, has, ironically, no cosy corners for the man who

merely wishes to practise his art in modest independence.

The only world open to such a man is, as I have said, Bohemia: a kind of Red Indian Reservation, whose inhabitants contrive to subsist by borrowing each other's money, sleeping in each other's basements, and coming in on each other's round of drinks. Thus one can roughly say that from the English upper-middle-classes and/or academically educated classes one can expect a wide scatter of talent. The way will be made smooth for even real *minor* talent. From the other and wider nation, we can look for the struggling and painful emergence of the occasional writer of extremely individual vision; the writer (like D. H. Lawrence, say), who is 'impossible', for whom 'nothing can be done', who will not 'fit in'. It is, of course, on his obstinate unconscious resistance to 'fitting in' that the power, originality, and usefulness of such a writer very largely depends. There are good poets (I have known a few) for whom 'society' can do nothing; and for whom even the individual can do very little, beyond letting them have a bed for the night sometimes, or giving them money which they will at once spend on drink.

4

I belong myself to the second generation of poets I have been discussing: the bohemian 'out-group' of the 1940s. It was a generation that, by 1945, felt itself as if stranded. 'Your whole generation,' I remember Empson saying to me about that time, in his vivid way, 'seems to me, as it were, *slugged*!' Yet at that very period, when the wartime boom in 'new poets' was being followed by a slump, certain calmer poets of an older generation were coming, for the first time, for a wide public, into their own. I am thinking particularly of the work of Dr. Edwin Muir, Mr. Robert Graves, and Miss Kathleen Raine. What gave these three poets their distinction, in the 1940s, to a younger writer like myself was that as poets they did not seem to depend—as so many of the new poets of the war years apparently had done—on the stimulus of outer event. Their work compelled one to revise the notion, so deeply ingrained into so many of us in the 1930s, of the poem as a *social product*: but neither did it fit in with the narrower notion, which might apply to many of the 'new romantic' writers of the 1940s, of the poem as a *psychological document*. Each of these poets sought for a group-transcending and self-transcending theme. Each found in ancient myths symbols of recurrent human dilemmas. Yet, though this poetry of deep symbolism had great distinction, it could not, of its very nature, have a notable sweep. For a poet like Miss Raine, for instance, Blake is automatically the greatest of poets because he is in the line of what she thinks the only valid philosophical tradition (the neo-Platonic tradition) and because he has seen farthest into the world of eternal forms; and yet one knows that there is a human sense in which he is not so great as, say, Shakespeare or Chaucer. Human everyday emotions cannot in the end be dismissed (as Miss Raine tends to dismiss them) as 'the transient'. And if we care only for the symbolic meanings in poetry, in the end we may find it handier to have the symbols *without* the poetry.

'Can there still be,' in the 1940s one wondered—admiring these three writers, but with the reservations I have indicated—'can there still be a poetry of the mixed, untidy, terribly dangerous but also warm,

human, and sometimes lovable world in which we live?
Or is it too late for that?' That question has an obvious
relevance to the wider question I have all this time been
obliquely discussing: the narrowing, and the specialization, of the audience.

5

I am still, in fact, in these apparently desultory reflections, pursuing a thread. Whatever limiting judgements
we may make on the *scope* of the three poets I have just
mentioned, many of us might agree that in their handling
of the primary medium—in the strictness and purity of
their diction, their abhorrence of vague, turbulent, or
affected language—they set a good example to younger
poets. They were Atticisers, going back to the older
chastity of our language, rather than Alexandrians,
attempting to enrich it from disparate and alien sources.
Ours has often, indeed, been described as an Alexandrian
age, and Alexandrianism is today often defended: Mr.
Auden for instance, attacking the Atticisers, mocks in a
recent poem at 'those critics'

> *Whose crude provincial gullets crave from books*
> *Plain cooking made still plainer by plain cooks. . . .*

Yet, with all respect, Mr. Auden is wrong. Bagehot when
he preferred, as something of a higher order, the severe
style of Wordsworth at his best to the ornate style of
Tennyson was not being 'crude' or 'provincial'; and a
concentration on surface ornament, in literature, as in
the visual arts, is very often a symptom of the decay of
the structural imagination.

To say this is not to dismiss, say, Bernini as a sculptor
or Mr. Wallace Stevens as a poet; it is to say, merely,

that the triumphs of the baroque must be triumphs of the second order; that the classical style in one sense (the severe and simple style) does remain the classical style in another (the style that we can go on safely taking as a model). Work which, with even minor success, conforms to certain canons of structural decorum can always teach us what these canons are; work which brilliantly breaks rules can have no direct progeny. This generalization applies in small things as in great. Palgrave noted that Shelley's line,

And wild / *roses*/ and iv/y serp/entine

has a peculiar beauty that comes from the daring reversion of the accent on the second, here italicized, foot. Sir Winston Churchill, when Sir Edward Marsh pointed out Palgrave's note to him, asked roguishly whether the beauty of the line would not become more 'peculiar' still, if it read:

And wild/ *roses*/ and serp/entine /*ivy*. . .

The answer, of course, is that the line, so altered, would be merely a mess; when the sensitive fifth foot, as well as the sensitive second foot, is reversed, it ceases to be metrical. Thus the daring of many innovating, Alexandrianly ornate modern poets lies in their successful departure from a norm, a central standard of usage; but these successful departures do not themselves become *new* norms, from which subsequent poets can equally daringly depart. Beyond the successful extreme of distortion, there lies mere shapelessness.

That is why Metaphysical periods in poetry are followed, not by yet more extravagant developments of the Metaphysical mode, but by reversions to Augustan simplicity. There is, throughout all literary history, a continuing process of corrective reaction. The taste for the pregnantly obscure, similarly, leads us in time to relish even an insipid plainness; after an overdose of Dylan Thomas, we might find ourselves delighting in Shenstone. And this process of corrective reaction does of course make it possible—Mr. Lehmann raised this point when I discussed an earlier draft of this essay with him—to discuss changes in literary fashions in idiom and diction to a considerable degree in abstraction from the social changes that may have accompanied them. A vivid interest in politics, for instance, among poets of the 1930s like Mr. Auden did not itself *directly* produce a wish to write poetry in a very direct, conversational style; the new interest, the new style were both parallel results of complex deeper causes. Similarly, Dylan Thomas's early poems do not seem very obscure when compared to Auden's more or less contemporary work *because* Thomas is turning his attention inward, to an inner turbulence; Thomas's language and his themes both reflect this broader process of corrective reaction—intuition and feeling, the more groping and tentative impulses of the mind, are asserting their rights against the poetry of concepts and of outward-turned perception.

Literary 'programmes', in fact, are merely rough generalizations—made by critics who are often 'failed poets'—from a whole set of more or less spontaneous shifts in idiom and interest. Groups of poets do not so much set out to do a new thing, as suddenly discover what sort of new thing it is that they are doing. The corrective reaction of the 1950s is, as I have said, in favour of the 'plain style'. But here again the notion of the medium in one of its secondary applications (the nature of the

117

audience) comes in. What aims, today, at being a new Augustan mode *might*, as I say, become a new academic mode: verse as a required accomplishment in junior lecturers. One teacher-poet of the newer generation, Mr. D. J. Enright—who has avoided and indeed disapproves of the prevailing Empsonian influence—is notable for the richness of his often straggling and untidy poems in bits of particularized observation and unashamedly direct expressions of humane feeling. Yet his poems are not so 'finished' as the poems, narrower in their scope, of somebody like Mr. Donald Davie; they have been described to me by a good judge as 'notes for poems'. The poet who rejects the fashionable mould may, in fact, never find any proper mould at all. Yet certainly in some other poets of Mr. Enright's generation the ironical tone becomes a trick. The clever young men are showing off to each other; the wider audience, the perhaps mythical 'common reader', is at the most allowed to overhear. 'Smart Alec slickness'—so the same judge described to me this tone. Irony becomes a mask for a lack of that assurance, which I have been insisting a poet needs; it defends the poet against the reader and also against himself—against an irritated awareness, sometimes, that his feelings are not adequate to a situation. Knowingness, self-consciousness, disguised callowness are the dangers of the new mode: respect for clarity, a striving for a balanced honesty of statement, are its elements of promise. It is good, at least, that young poets should be again ready to generalize, to moralize, to explore and question accepted values. There, perhaps, lies the bridge from the university audience to the wider public.

6

I may seem to have been concerned rather drearily
with the swing of the pendulum: from the clear to the
obscure, from the public to the private, from the statement to the image, from the plain to the ornate, from
the dry to the wet, and now back again. One should note,
however, that some tendencies over our period have not
been reversed: for instance, the tendency away (since about
1930) from free verse to regular forms, flexibly handled,
and the similar tendency away from extremely elliptical
and allusive writing—the 'cultural rock-jumping style'
of Mr. Pound's *Cantos*, say—back towards a more
traditional articulation of the poem. These tendencies
are hopeful ones, in relation to the problem of the
audience. So is the support that poetry receives from
official bodies like the B.B.C. and the Arts Council and
from unofficial bodies like the Institute of Contemporary
Arts and the Apollo Society, which has done so much to
raise the standard of public readings of poetry, and to
introduce audiences all over the country to new work.
All this, of course, is encouragement from the top down;
for some poets, it may have the taint of bureaucracy about
it. I should certainly like to see the wider public spontaneously arranging its own poetry readings, clamouring in
the bookshops for new volumes of poetry, writing to the
B.B.C. to say that not enough poetry is heard. But I do
not expect to see this: ours, alas, is not a 'grass-roots'
culture. What official, or semi-official, encouragement of
poetry *can* do is to build into our society a system of
checks against the triumph of merely commercial stan-

dards. And while these checks are working, there are
children at school and there are students at evening
classes who, given enough sensitivity and enthusiasm
from teachers, form the nucleus of a potentially quite
wide audience for poetry. There, our hope lies.

When I look about me, among the younger poets, I
do not see any dominating figure; I see an abundant
variety of minor talent. For language—for language as
the wider medium on which the great poet ultimately
draws—this may not be a bad thing. In the poetry of the
younger people what one notices especially is a growing
'unity of tone'—by which I don't exactly mean that
any of them might have written any of the others'
poems—and also a growing attempt to revive standards
of clarity and correctness. Clarity and correctness are not
in themselves wildly exciting ideals; but the acceptance
of definite standards, valid so far as they go, by minor
writers gives the major writer, when he comes, something firm to build on.

It is on the language, I think, so far as we have managed to preserve it in health, to 'keep up English'—it
is on the language, and not on any definite foreseeable
system of ideas—that the major poet, when he comes,
will build. We rightly fought, during the Second World
War, to preserve the liberal society. And it is, ironically,
of the very nature of the liberal society that it has no
unifying philosophy or vision; it does not, like some
archaic societies (which, for the mass of mankind, must
have been much more disagreeable to live in) distil its
own poetry. Yet the liberal society may have a unifying
tone. And the language of poetry—so much 'the true
language of feeling', so much the language of obscure
tact—may both make it clearer to us what that precious

tone is, and help to fertilize the tone and to preserve it. That is why 'values' and 'manners' can never be irrelevant concerns even for the most discontented and radical of young poets.

The Author
and the Theatre

T. C. WORSLEY

T HE VERY TITLE raises the issue at once: the two
terms of it live in an absurdly uneasy relationship.
The Theatre notoriously distrusts the Author
whenever he appears there; and the Author—unless he is
that special brand called 'playwright' (which is somehow something quite distinct) seems to regard the Theatre
as a thing essentially frivolous and not to be taken
seriously like the Novel, the Biography and the rest of
his categories. How different it is in contemporary France!
There, if a man has made a reputation as a novelist or a
poet, he is immediately wooed by the Theatre. Or perhaps
it is simply that, in the cultural climate prevailing there,
the Theatre beckons to him. Anyhow, in France writing
plays is a branch of literature at which he will naturally
try his hand. Here it is not so. The Theatre is so far from
wooing those who make a reputation in other fields that
when a distinguished novelist and short story writer like
Mr. Angus Wilson writes a play, it is left to a provincial
repertory company to give it its first hearing. And so far
are we from the position when the Theatre naturally
beckons to the Author that our leading novelists never

even seem to remember it as a possible medium. Our leading Men of Letters don't much patronize the Theatre; it hardly comes into their surveys of literature. It is a separate activity.

The divorce between Literature and the Theatre is one of the saddest phenonema of English Letters. Fortunately it is not complete, and there is some evidence, as we shall presently see, for hoping that the two may make it up. Already the poets at least have made a bridge across the gulf, and the stage—Mr. Eliot is here the pioneer—is accepted both by managements, actors *and* audiences as one of the proper platforms of poetry. And Mr. Grahame Greene may yet have opened a gap through which other novelists may flock. Managements profess themselves to be starved for plays of quality; it may one day strike them that the practising novelist is as likely to produce one for them as an unfledged stage-struck undergraduate. They may have the sense to try to lure the practised writer in: and the practised writers may discover the pleasures and advantages of the dramatic form and find the Theatre beckoning to them.

How, in the land of Shakespeare, this cleavage has arisen would take a longer time to analyse than we have here. Of course, the divorce has never been absolute, though the communication between the two has never, since the eighteenth century, been easy. Periodically serious attempts are made to heal the breach. Perhaps the most promising of all of these was that associated with the Court Theatre and Granville Barker in the 1900's. Barker had the luck to coincide with Bernard Shaw and the combination of an author of genius and a producer of exceptional talent and integrity produced a momentary reconciliation. While leaning heavily on Bernard

Shaw as the star attraction, Barker did everything he could to draw other literary talent into his theatre. He was only partly successful. Galsworthy's and his own were perhaps the only English names that were added to the potential repertoire. But others at least tried their hands. A beginning was made. If the Great War had not arrived to snuff it out, the venture might have won through its financial difficulties and the foundations might have been laid for a permanent repertory of some kind.

For Granville Barker's main objective was to establish the repertory habit, instead of, or at least alongside of, the commercial 'long run'. And this was not only because the commercial long run creates conditions where it is virtually impossible for the actors to practice their craft as an art. He was also shrewd enough to see that only under a repertory scheme could the theatre display itself continuously and consistently as a form of art deserving the same respect and support as any other. This is as true today as it was then. But what became clear, even before the war came, and even in the much less stringent economic conditions obtaining before the Great War, was that repertory was too costly a venture for private enterprise. Without the subsidies which, in all continental countries, the State supplied, it could not finance itself. Unfortunately before this could be definitively established, the outbreak of the Great War cut short the whole venture.

When the war was over the theatre resumed its haphazard commercial routine. Light sophistication became the dominating mode. Mr. Noel Coward, theatrical to his fingertips, became the type author and though, Mr. Coward might accept the appellation author, he would hardly perhaps be at home in the Profession of

Letters. The twenties seem in retrospect, an age of the commercial theatre run riot. Of course, there were at the same time contrary movements. At the tiny Gate Theatre founded by Peter Godfrey the latest experiments in Continental Theatre could be enjoyed by those with a mind to it; the Old Vic, taking up Granville Barker's ideas, played a fairly wide repertory which put the Russians alongside Shakespeare. And Mr. Terence Gray at Cambridge established a little theatre where the most advanced experiments in technique were carried out. But what we see—and it is sad to see—is the growing split in our culture showing itself in the theatre too. The theatre might, with better luck, or better management, have proved the meeting place where high and middle and low brow met, where the split might be healed. But in the inter-war years it could not resist the pressure. The small theatre and minority audiences were adopting Ibsen and Chekhov into the accepted repertoire. The large theatre and the majority audiences were gobbling the soufflés offered them by Mr. Noel Coward, Mr. Frederick Lonsdale or the musical comedy specialists. Bernard Shaw—an exception to any general rule and very much an author in every sense—turned more and more after *St. Joan* in the early twenties, to the political conversaziones, and had surprisingly little influence and few, if any, followers. There were a few professional playwrights of quality. There was Mr. Sean O'Casey; and in the thirties two notable recruits to the Drama were James Bridie and J. B. Priestley. It would, of course, be an exaggeration to stigmatize the inter-war period as a barren one. But undoubtedly it was a thin one for the theatre. And it was not only thin in authorship, it was thin, too, in its own special techniques and arts.

One might put the situation a little dramatically by saying that in the inter-war years the professional theatre itself was still in the grip of the du Maurier naturalism. The leading lights of the profession, the admired actors and actresses, were those most skilled in the art of drawing-room comedy. To light a cigarette as nonchalantly as Sir George or to pour tea with the effortless charm of Miss Vanburgh, this, for the acting profession, was at that time success in life. The very special artificial technique of drawing room comedy and naturalistic drama engaged as little of the author's talents as it did of the actors'. Especially the author had to suppress the whole range of vocabulary and of verbal music. What was required of him was half sentences and monosyllables cunningly arranged. And the players, expert in timing and in slipping over these interjections as adroitly as possible, were content to let their style stop at that. In these conditions it was obviously true that the playwright's was a very specialized technique and one which would not tempt those who did not find in themselves the flair for this particular and limited way of writing.

While the theatre, then, as a professional entity was content to maintain itself on a purely frivolous basis, it could hardly complain if it was accepted on its own valuation. Individuals and minorities battled nobly to plant the flag of a more respectable theatre and to keep it flying, and as we shall see with some success. But in the theatre less than anywhere do minorities and individuals count. The individuals and the minorities had their successes and in the long run they are likely to tell. In the long run, it is such that are remembered—The Lyric Hammersmith of Nigel Playfair, the Everyman, the Gate, the Arts, the Malvern Festival. But so long as they remained unrecognized minorities and the theatre as a professional body remained dedicated to the purely frivolous, so long was the serious author who had not yet attempted the drama justified in feeling that the theatre was not for him.

The theatre was in danger of being, if it had not indeed become, a specialist activity outside the provinces of authors in other fields.

2

Since the war however, this feeling has no longer been justified. A change, and a very complete change, has come over the theatre. It might be symbolized, once again, by the kind of actor and actress who is now at the head of the profession. The light comedians and the du Maurier naturalists still have their popularity, but their place is no longer at the head of the hierarchy. Only those who have proved themselves in the classical and, above all, in the great Shakespearean roles can now be candidates for that position: and the theatre and the public recognize this as just. It is only a small thing, but it is the first step in the theatre's rehabilitation.

Perhaps the most important thing that has come about since the war (of course, it has actually been a gradual process now come to maturity) is that the theatre as a body for the first time since his own day has a responsible attitude toward Shakespeare. This is already a more considerable beginning than it may appear on the surface. The world of letters has down the centuries had good reason to despise our Shakespearean Theatre. The eighteenth century simply re-wrote or re-arranged the texts to suit their own confident good taste, while the nineteenth dropped whole passages from the plays and whole plays from the repertoire in the interest of their prudery. It was not until William Poel, and then after him Granville Barker, that due respect began to be paid to the texts, and that Shakespearean production deserved to be treated honourably as a branch of letters. Now the outlook of these pioneers is widespread. Now the theatre does deserve to be treated in this respect seriously as a form of art and to be accepted by the world of letters and scholarship on an equal footing. The gain, incidentally, to scholarship will be (as it has indeed already been) considerable. Shakespeare after all cannot be understood simply in the study. He comes to full life only on the stage; and a scholar like Mr. Dover Wilson has testified for instance, that the production of the four histories by Stratford in Coronation year materially illuminated his view of the plays and their meaning.

The pioneering in this changed attitude towards Shakespeare goes back to the turn of the century to William Poel and his Elizabethan Society and to Granville Barker. If William Poel with his devotion to the text and the proper way of speaking the verse set the movement going, it was Granville Barker who moved it out of the sphere of the 'cranky' into the practical world of full-scale theatre, and, in that arena, opposed the ideal of responsible producer's Shakespeare to the actor-manager's travesty of the real thing. And when after the first war, he himself went out of practice as an active producer, his ideals were preserved and his principles practised at the Old Vic. Mr. Harcourt Williams, especially, during a bleak period, nurtured the tradition there. And not only were the plays presented in something like the form he could recognize as his own, but the school of actors and actresses who are now the leader of the profession were all trained in their practice there. Sir John Gielgud, Sir Laurence Olivier, Michael Redgrave, Dame Edith Evans, Miss Peggy Ashcroft, to mention no others, went through the classical mill there between the wars. Sir John Gielgud deserves particular mention. In two famous seasons at the Old Vic he established himself—at an absurdly early age—as our leading young Shakespearean actor, but then instead of relapsing, as was the common habit, back into the commercial round, he stormed the commercial theatre with his classical fare and succeeded in convincing the managements that Shakespeare not only entertained but paid. The decision, one might say, was imposed on Sir John because his particular kind of poetic and romantic acting could only express itself by means of the classics since there were no playwrights at that time writing the kind of thing which would give just expression to his gifts.

Thus, when, after the second war, the time came to consolidate the impetus which that war had given to the serious theatre, there was already a decent tradition of production on which to build and a fine crop of actors and actresses, and producers, too, trained in a good school. In the first flush of enthusiasm the situation looked rosy. Stratford, captured by an enterprising young band, roused itself out of its provincial sleep and took its place as a leading centre of Shakespearan production, and the Old Vic led by Sir Laurence Olivier and Sir Ralph Richardson seemed to be making a bid for the position of unofficial National Theatre.

Certainly the position has somewhat slipped since then, simply because there is no central organization by which the work can be continued. The Old Vic has relapsed into

K 129

what one must regard as its rightful position, that of a *Volkstheater*. Stratford, it is true, maintains its position, and in the provinces the leading repertory companies keep up something as near the Granville Barker standard as their very limited resources allow; while the commercial theatre is still prepared from time to time to mount seasons of repertory on a limited scale in the Granville Barker manner. But organizationally the position is precarious: for the success won is dependent on a very uncertain economic position. Yet, however much we may quarrel with individual productions and particular producers, whatever shortcomings there still are in our approach to Shakespeare and the classics, it is at least true to say now that the theatre has a responsible attitude to them and deserves in return to be treated seriously.

3

The acceptance, then, by the theatre of its responsibilities towards the classics, and Shakespeare in particular, and the recognition by the world of letters of that acceptance is a good beginning. But new work is the life blood of any art and here the picture is slightly less encouraging, though by no means without hope. The hope comes from the fact that plays which in the inter-war years would almost certainly have been seen only in the minority theatre have been staged instead in the commercial theatre and have won for themselves a wide audience, and, most strikingly, this has happened with the plays of two poets, T. S. Eliot and Christopher Fry, at a time when in the purely literary world poetry might seem to be in a moribund or, at least, a very quiescent state. The poets have, of course, turned up intermittently in the theatre during the last twenty-five years. But it is only since the war, it seems to me, that a climate in which they have really felt themselves welcomed has prevailed—and in the majority, not merely the minority, theatre. The foundations of this change of heart were being laid, of course, just before the war at the same time that Sir John Gielgud was bringing the classics to the commercial theatre.

In the late thirties a very whole hearted attempt was made to close the gap between literature and the theatre, notably by the Group Theatre under the direction of Mr. Rupert Doone. The Group Theatre set out to divert some of the abundant energy of the literary movement of the time on to the stage, and with some success. The leading writers of the movement all, with this opportunity there before them, turned their hands to playwriting. The best remembered of these plays are the collaborations between Auden and Isherwood. But they were not the only ones. Both Stephen Spender and Louis MacNeice made their first dramatic attempts for the Group Theatre. It is a sad thing that this experiment, so promising for the relations between the theatre and literature, should have died with the war, as Granville Barker's died in the Great War; and that attempts to revive it afterwards have never come to anything. In retrospect it must be admitted that the actual achievements of the Group were not lasting. None of the plays which it brought to birth has stayed in the repertory except *The Ascent of F. 6* and, perhaps, *The Dog Beneath the Skin*, which is occasionally revived by enterprising Groups. And none of the authors have really been successfully lured into the theatre. But this is surely because the war cut short the experiment before it had had time fully to establish itself. It was not to be hoped that after so long a time of divorce between the theatre and literature, the division could be healed all in a moment. But the Group did bring together the two parties into what seemed then an alliance full of promise both for poetry and the theatre and but for the war something lasting might have come out of it.

It was from a parallel movement that the present revival originated, a movement for theatre in the Church, of which Mr. Martin Browne was the director. It was he who persuaded Mr. T. S. Eliot to write a play for performance in Canterbury Cathedral, and it was this play, *Murder in the Cathedral*, which really opened up the possibility of bringing poetry into the theatre once again. For not only was *Murder in the Cathedral* found to be as successful in the theatre as in the Church but it encouraged Mr. Eliot to continue with what many people (myself included) think of as his best play, *Family Reunion*. Neither play found a very wide public, though *Family Reunion* did tempt Sir John Gielgud with its main part and only recently The Old Vic produced *Murder in the Cathedral* with great success. But at least the movement spread and Mr. Ashley Dukes ran his little Mercury Theatre at Nottinghill Gate as a theatre devoted to the Poetic Drama for a year or two, discovering at least two plays which went into the European repertory, *Happy as Larry* and Ronald Duncan's *This Way to the Tomb*.

It was after the war with the Shakespearean revival in full swing that poetry really captured—if only, it seems, for a spell—the majority theatre. Mr. Eliot's *The Cocktail Party* caught the fancy of larger audiences both here and in the States; and then Mr. Christopher Fry whose first plays had also been written for performance in Church, was discovered when Sir John Gielgud saw his *The Lady's not for Burning* at the Arts, promptly bought it and staged it in a superb production which was an immediate and resounding success in the commercial theatre. If Mr. Eliot had been the only poetic success of this period it might have been passed over as an accident; all the more so because in *The Cocktail Party* Mr. Eliot abandoned the dramatic form he had been developing in his earlier plays in favour of a different one which, deliberately or accidently, made considerable concessions to the commercial theatre. In the two earlier plays he had used, roughly speaking, the form of Greek tragedy complete with chorus and his own idiosyncratic verse. In *The Cocktail Party* he reversed the process and taught himself to use the ordinary workaday technical framework of the day before yesterday's domestic comedy, trying to make that carry his deeper meanings; this necessarily meant a very ascetic use of verse: so much so that Mr. Eliot himself has remarked in his *Poetry and Drama* 'it is an open question whether there is any poetry in the play at all.'

But if Mr. Eliot's new approach squeezed the poetry too thin, there are some who feel that Mr. Christopher Fry squeezed the poetry in too thick. Since I am not concerned with literary—dramatic criticism here, I needn't defend him against them. The point, for our purpose, is that the poetry, however one might estimate it, is certainly thick enough on the ground in Mr. Fry's plays and this made it clear that poetry was what audiences, for the time being at least, wanted from the theatre. Equally, it was what actors and all engaged in the theatre wanted too. For the average naturalistic piece, however good, only calls out from the craftsmen in the theatre a limited portion of their talents. It denies the actor half the range of his voice; it limits the fantasy of the designer, and it fetters the imagination of the producer. In the theatre of today when Shakespeare is the most popular of authors and where the best of our actors and actresses have been trained in the classical school, the demand from the theatre itself is for a very different kind of writing. All our leading actors and actresses want modern plays; but they want plays which are really *written*, plays with language in them, into which they can get their teeth as they can with Shakespeare, plays with enough rhetoric and poetry in them for them to get their tongues round. That is what they want and what they too seldom find. Authors have not followed this change, this switch round in taste, and either still shy off the drama as a medium too limited for them, or still supply emasculated texts in flaccid prose of the old kind.

Not that I am by any means making a special plea for poetry in the theatre. It seems to me at least debatable whether poetry is indeed a form of writing appropriate to the contemporary world. But there is, as Mr. Cocteau has reminded us, a poetry *of* the theatre which is no less important and exciting and which does bring into play the full resources of both actors and technicians on the one hand, and of authors on the other. I suppose of all playwrights practising today M. Anouilh is the one who exemplifies this quality most clearly, and he is an author who commands as popular a following in England as he does in France. But the general impression—too often fostered by our critics—that we can supply almost nothing in the way of plays is grossly misleading. Here, as so often, we underestimate ourselves. The complaint is often heard that we are coming to rely entirely on the French for our plays; and yet at the very same time the French are complaining that the Paris Theatres are filled with English plays; and it is a fact that the German Theatre self-confessedly depends on our playwrights to keep itself supplied. The English Theatre is not so despised abroad as it is at home.

It must be admitted that there is not an equivalent amount of writing talent going into the theatre as into, say, the novel at the moment. But owing to having no national repertory theatre which means that a play once 'off' is almost never heard of again, there seems to be even less than in fact there is. For I must not seem to imply that there is very little writing talent in the theatre just because I feel there could be more. On the contrary there is much more than is generally recognized. I suggest that it would be possible to mount not one but four or five repertory seasons drawn from the plays of living English dramatists alone which would stand up well to an equivalent offering either from the poets or the novelists. We should be able to draw on (at the very least) the plays of: Sean O'Casey (at least two of which have yet to be performed professionally in London): of T. S. Eliot; of J. B. Priestley; of Christopher Fry, Charles Morgan, Terence Rattigan, Peter Ustinov, John Whiting, Denis Cannan, Owen Holder. And I name here only the professional playwrights who regularly produce plays for the theatre and whose plays are regularly sought for and regularly performed in continental repertories.

Such is the general ignorance, even in literary circles, of the theatre, that I am prepared to believe that the last three names in my list are known only to a very

small number of people. Yet Mr. Whiting, three of
whose plays (*Penny for a Song*, *Saints Day* and *Marching
Song*) have been seen in London, is a playwright every
bit as serious, interesting and original as Mr. John Wain
is a novelist; Mr. Denis Cannan is quite as brilliant a
comic observer of his own day as Mr. Kingsley Amis;
and Mr. Owen Holder (*Facts of the Heart* and *A Kind
of Folly*) is as 'promising' an author as any of our
'promising' young novelists.

Yet, with our theatre organized as it is on a predominantly commercial basis, we must also admit the
frustrations and difficulties which authors who do try to
go to meet it come up against. The theatre does not make
it easy for authors. Yet it does seem to me that since the
war we have begun to see the development of a climate
in which the rift might be healed. The altogether more
adult attitude of the theatre towards Shakespeare; the
welcome given by audiences as well as actors and producers to poetry in the theatre; the popular success of
serious plays like Miss Bridget Boland's *The Prisoner* or
Mr. Grahame Greene's *The Living Room*; and the
establishment in a few of the big provincial centres of
repertory companies of high standards both in production
and choice of plays, all these things together, create the
kind of climate in which the theatre has a chance of
taking its place on an equality with the other arts.
Whether, in the absence of any form of organization
which can consolidate the ground won, the advance will
continue or not, is open to some doubt. And that—creat-
ing some form of organization—seems to me to be the
next important step.

4

The question that poses itself is really this. Is the time coming at last when we are going to be able to accept the theatre as a form of art deserving as much support and serious interest as any other? For the fact is that, broadly and generally speaking, it has not in the past been so accepted; it has been excluded from the brotherhood as a really not quite respectable member of the family. There have been faults clearly on both sides. But that era, as I have attempted to show, is passing, if it has not passed. In the transition period the theatre needs—I do not say it always welcomes—support, advice, help from the rest of the brotherhood. But what needs changing essentially is the attitude which is prepared to allow the theatre to exist in a separate compartment of our cultural life.

If, for instance, we had a National Theatre playing a regular repertory on the South Bank, its standards would be a matter of general and public concern. If the productions became shoddy, pressure would be brought to bear (in the various devious ways that pressure can be brought to bear in England) to raise them. The standards of that theatre and the choice of plays and so on would be matters of common discussion and common concern. One might even in the literary journals find the theatre discussed on an equality with literature and the fine arts.

I can see a great many objections to a National Theatre. I see a great many practical difficulties in the way of establishing one, and so far they have proved insuperable (it is not I think only money which prevents the National Theatre being established). But overriding all the objections and the obstacles is the simple fact that with its establishment the theatre would be at least officially

recognized as an art and, *far more important*, would be
perpetually on show as such. At the moment this is just
what it is not. There is in London, this great capital of
ours, no theatre which shows a permanent repertory
of the theatre classics—our own and other people's. It
is really an astonishing fact, this, when we compare the
situation with, say, Germany where every sizeable town
boasts a resident repertory company performing this task.

And the sad thing is that this gap bears most hardly
on the theatre as a living activity. One can see Shakespeare often enough in London, and we have revivals in
the commercial theatre and elsewhere of a few of the
favourite eighteenth-century comedies and of the plays of
Ibsen, Chekhov and so on. We are not absolutely starved
of the classics. But what about the plays meriting serious
consideration which have had their run—long or short—
and are then rarely if ever seen again?

We have in our native repertory alone a very considerable body of work that is simply overlooked by
default and which ought to be there on show, year in
and year out keeping before our eyes the very solid
achievement of our dramatists in the last forty or fifty
years. The best of Galsworthy's plays are much better
than the present estimate of him allows. Any of Granville
Barker's own plays would, I believe, give a most interesting evening in the theatre. Only a very limited
number of Shaw's plays are now revived, and then only
at long intervals. Are Drinkwater, Maugham, St. John
Ervine, Barrie, Laurence Housman, all just so much
waste? It seems to me improbable, even if they are for
the moment out of fashion. But there is, in the present
scheme of things, no way of telling. I should like to know
about some of the plays highly praised before the war.

Would they still stand up? Consider this list for instance: *After October* (Rodney Ackland), *Johnson over Jordan* (J. B. Priestley), *The Anatomist* (James Bridie), *Musical Chairs* (Rodney Ackland), *The Moon on the Yellow River* (Denis Johnston), *The World of Light* (Aldous Huxley). I pick these out at random as works highly praised by intelligent people at the time and which have simply fallen into the great vacuum of oblivion. It may be justly or it may be not. There is no way of knowing because there is—since there is no National Theatre—no machinery for reviving them: no machinery for mounting a modern repertoire, and so keeping the picture of the Theatre as a living art before our eyes. And this process of oblivion is going on all the time, is sucking plays down with itself month by month and year by year. When shall we next see in London *The Confidential Clerk* or *The Living Room*? They have had their run, and they have been trundled away and that, as far as they are concerned, is that. It may be argued that if they deserve to live they will, and that is no doubt true. But it is not the point. Even those which don't deserve to live deserve, many of them, a longer life than simply this London 'run' and their productions in the higher class reps afterwards. And the very fact that they are rarely, if ever, seen again gives to our whole view of the theatre an even greater feeling of transience, of ephemerality, than the form, already ephemeral, justifies. Let us suppose a lively national repertory company keeping before our eyes the worthwhile plays of yesterday and today from Shaw and Galsworthy through Bridie and Priestley to Eliot and Fry; and wouldn't then the theatre seem less of an off-and-on will-o-the-wisp and more a living force to which all writers and all authors might feel themselves drawn?

The New Criticism

L. D. LERNER

WHY DISCUSS LITERARY criticism in a symposium on *The Craft of Letters*? Is it not a quite separate craft, no more requiring literary ability than the judicious spectator need be able to play football himself? What does the adjective mean in the phrase 'literary criticism': does it mean (on the analogy of 'art criticism') criticism about literature? Or does it also mean criticism that is itself literary, that, since it uses the same medium as its subject-matter, bears a closer relation to it than art criticism does to art, and is itself part of literature? Is the critical activity something like the creative?

There are two main views on this: that criticism and creation are very different and even hostile; or that they are so similar that only poets make good critics. Oddly enough, both views are sometimes held by the same person, since either will do as a stick to beat critics with. The first is certainly false, and T. S. Eliot wrote *The Use of Poetry and the Use of Criticism* largely to dispose of it:

It is sometimes thought that criticism flourishes most when creative vigour is in defect. . . . Several gross assumptions underlie this prejudice, including a confusion between several different things, and between works of very different

140

quality, included under "criticism". . . . I affirm that there is a significant relation between the best poetry and the best criticism of the same period.

It is not only that there is nothing in one activity to inhibit the other: they actually overlap. The spectacle of F. R. Leavis scrutinizing a poem, say of Hardy's, to pounce on the words that display a flaw in attitude, is not all that different from Hardy revising his own poem; and a feeling not only for what has been done with words but for what can be done with them gives to the criticism of William Empson a quality that can only be called creative.

What of the other view: that the critical ability is a kind of by-product of the poetic, and that every great critic has been a poet. 'Pay no attention', wrote Ezra Pound, 'to the criticism of men who have never themselves written a notable work.' If you look at the great critics of the past, you see that this view is obviously true: Sidney, Ben Jonson, Dryden, Johnson, Coleridge and Arnold were all poets. When we turn to this century the difference is striking: Bradley, Middleton Murry, Richards, Leavis and a large number of Americans, who have published neither novels nor poetry, are so obviously critics of distinction that one can only conclude that something new must have happened to criticism— not only is there more of it, but more people, and more sorts of people, are doing it. This has been often remarked in Britain, and has in fact led to the suggestion that all this is improper, a mark of decadence and Alexandrianism. In other countries the situation varies: perhaps the only one where the flood is greater than here is the United States. The New Criticism (as it is there called: we have been too bewildered to give it a name here, and I have had to borrow theirs) tends to be more fanatical than ours, more ingenious, and much more extensive: and at its rare best, more exciting. It also seems to have kept in closer touch with creative writing, so that many of its leading practitioners are themselves poets or novelists: John Crowe Ransom, Allen Tate, Robert Penn Warren, Lionel Trilling, R. P. Blackmur, Ivor Winters. This essay is confined to criticism in England, and the comparison with other countries is left to readers to draw for themselves; and my method will be to try and impose some order on our English bewilderment by asking what the aim of criticism is. I suggest that it has two minor and two major aims. Terminology is difficult in this matter, and the terms I suggest are rather arbitrary: the first two I shall call the social and the pragmatic, the others the practical and the theoretical.

By the social function of criticism I mean the building up of prestige and enthusiasm. It is important that literature should matter: that new books should be looked forward to, should (to put it at its lowest) be discussed in polite conversation. Even the most dedicated writer and his most enthusiastic readers can be cheered up by the feeling that they are at least noticed. We may call this the Sunday-paper view of criticism: the Bloomsbury circle discussed by Mr. Paul Bloomfield have perhaps done it better than anyone, though at their best, as he is at pains to point out, they did much more, of course. Something very similar to this has been done by popular academics like Sir Arthur Quiller-Couch: to read Q's essays is to hear someone telling you how much he likes literature, and obviously telling the truth; and insofar as this sets people reading, it is wholly admirable. But though it is distasteful and irresponsible to despise this criticism, to

take it too seriously would be equally mistaken. To be
effective, Sunday-paper criticism does not need to be
good; to show how much you have enjoyed a book, you
do not need to have much to say about it. Indeed, to lay
too much stress on enthusiasm has its dangers, for it can
turn so easily into bluster. Communicating zest is so very
personal, that perhaps it should be confined to personal
contacts; and the view that even this social function is
best served by paying the reader the compliment of
assuming that he wants serious criticism, though harsh
and impracticable, is quite understandable.

By the pragmatic function I mean a guide to the actual
practice of writing. The Elizabethans used to write hand-
books like George Gascoigne's *Certain Notes*, aiming to
'lend you instructions towards the making of English
verse or rhyme'. No reputable critic would do this
today; and we cannot help smiling at Gascoigne's advice
'to help you a little with rhyme, work thus: when you
have set down your first verse, take the last word thereof
and count o'er all the words of the self-same sound by
order of the alphabet'. In order not to be mechanical,
'advice' of this sort has of course to be specific, directed
at a particular writer's particular problem, and so is
never likely to see print. In America this is institutional-
ized in creative writing classes, at which the English are
inclined to smile as they smile at Gascoigne: perhaps too
hastily.

What is important, however, is the indirectly pragmatic. A great deal of criticism which takes the form of
comment on existing texts has as its aim, or one of its
aims, the improvement of literature as yet unwritten.
Thus Donald Davie says of his *Purity of Diction in
English Verse* (which is mainly about the eighteenth

century), 'it is to the would-be poet of today that I should like to address myself'. I am not sure that he has really done this, or that his book would be any better if he had; but the remark shows a healthy concern for the influence of criticism on poetry. The leading examples of this sort of practitioner-critic are Ezra Pound and T. S. Eliot. Almost everything of value that Pound did has been as much concerned with the future of poetry as its present and past: this is true not only of his prose but of much of his verse, from *Hugh Selwyn Mauberley* to his translation of *The Seafarer*, monstrous as a poem but admirable as a hint. Eliot will be discussed later in this essay; here I must remark how much of his criticism is sharpened by the fellow-craftsman's interest, the look-out for what might be useful: not only in such obvious reflections on his trade as *Poetry and Drama*, but in his early work on the metaphysicals and the Elizabethans, where the concern is more for the future of poetry in general than of his own in particular. He may have understood these writers better than those whose reading of them had been more disinterested. But of this more later.

Now to the two major functions, both of which are covered by the American term New Criticism. I call them two, though the distinction is worth drawing largely as a way of tracing their interrelations. Criticism as appreciation is an attempt to show what is happening in actual works of literature and so (the corollary is inevitable) to judge it. The critic in this sense is merely the sensitive and discriminating reader who is also articulate; and the aim of his criticism is pedagogic, in that it is designed to help less acute readers. This is practical criticism; if there is any 'one true aim' of criticism it is this. But there is no doubt that a great deal of criticism aims at something more (or at any rate, something other): an examination of the very nature of literature. To reflect upon this, not as a means to understanding and responding to actual books, but as a disinterested philosophical activity, is as natural, and as proper, as to reflect upon the nature of science, or history, or thinking. *Practical* criticism, in short, asks: What is this book about, and is it good? *Theoretical* criticism asks: What is literature? Now it is obvious that these activities overlap and interact. In the first place the theoretical critic must be able to appreciate literature and (this disposes of many a philosopher) be able to show his literary experience by its presence in his work. If he writes a book that begins by asking What is Art, and works in towards applications and actual poems, we call his work Aesthetics; but he may equally well begin with a method similar to that of the practical critic, though with a different aim, and work outwards towards his generalization—this will be the reflective litterateur rather than the literary philosopher. And equally the practical critic will on occasion find himself bumping against theoretical questions, finding that to make up his mind about a poem he has to make up his mind about poetry. The reason why practical criticism in the more limited sense has such scope is that this happens so seldom: there is much to be done without squabbling over what literature is (a matter on which we often agree when we don't stop to argue it out), simply by careful reading and sensitive exposition.

This distinction is useful as a way of talking about the work of F. R. Leavis and his followers. Leavis is the supreme example of a practical critic. He has always resisted the suggestion that he should elaborate in general

L

terms the bases of his criticism, which he considers a cruder, less valuable activity than the close scrutiny of actual texts; and insofar as it is a judgement on his own powers the resistance is wise, for it is in this latter activity that he excels. The opinion is more than this, of course; the pedagogic aim is never far from Leavis' mind, and he is surely right in believing that it is more important to train young men to appreciate literature than to reflect upon its nature. The emphasis on 'training to read' is one that has aroused some opposition. Everyone agrees that literature is—has always been—appreciated only by a minority; and this view of criticism implies a minority within that minority—the very small group who can respond and judge of themselves instructing the larger, but still small, group who can respond when shown. This idea is disturbing to our democratic prejudices; this need not mean that it is wrong, but anyone who seems to *want* it to be true is obviously going to be unpopular.

The work of Leavis was published almost exclusively in *Scrutiny*, the periodical that he inspired and helped to edit from 1932 to its death in 1953; and has been expanded and reprinted in a steady stream of books. *New Bearings in English Poetry* was a pioneer work, and gave a spirited and intelligent defence of Eliot, Pound and Hopkins, but it bears rereading less than any of Leavis' other work. *Revaluation* attempts to re-assess English poetry in the light of the twentieth century achievement, moving the Romantics away from the centre of the picture (though 3 of its 6 essays are devoted to them). The book does not hang together completely and is of mixed quality: the attack on Milton seems to me to deserve its notoriety, but much of the rest is excellent and all is intelligent. *The Great Tradition* may be his best work.

Leavis locates the great tradition of the English novel in Jane Austen, George Eliot, James and Conrad, and the book is a study of the last three: he is brilliant in his account of their greatness, and ruthless in his insistence on the inferiority of all others.

To describe Leavis' view of literature in general terms is something he has himself refused to do, so it seems an arrogance to attempt a summing up. But one can at least remark two obvious preferences, for wit and intelligence in poetry over the romantic swoon, and for moral passion and vitality over 'art' (Donne rather than Shelley, Lawrence rather than Flaubert). He shares with Lawrence a conviction that the modern world is sick, a conviction that was seen more and more strongly in the tone of *Scrutiny* as the years passed. There are legitimate and illegitimate reasons for holding this; and in Lawrence sometimes, in Leavis often, the latter seem to predominate.

None of Leavis' collaborators and disciples in *Scrutiny* is as eminent as he, though in the few essays of James Smith there are signs of a mind of even finer distinction. There is also L. C. Knights, whose *Drama and Society in the Age of Jonson* is a gallant attempt to link some very good literary criticism with some very good economic history.

Leavis has been influenced by both of the two great seminal minds of modern criticism, T. S. Eliot and I. A. Richards. Richards too is a practical critic, if we may take his approach in *Interpretation in Teaching* as representative; but it is not wholly representative, for Richards has done very little actual criticism, and most of that as illustrations to his long and frequent discussions of what criticism is and how it should be done. He has tended, too, to mix criticism with other disciplines—psychology, semantics and linguistic analysis. This adulteration makes much of Richards' work heavy going for the merely literary, and when he himself admits that his psychology is heterodox one wonders if it is worth the effort to master the jargon or follow the arguments. There must of course be peacemakers between the arts and the sciences nowadays, and even though the treaty can take other forms than that proposed by Richards, his must be respected as a brave and intelligent reaction to the modern world. But his best work is more directly related to literature than this, and its distinction is beyond question. It is to be seen in *Practical Criticism*. This book begins as the record of an experiment in reading among Cambridge undergraduates in the twenties: a dozen poems were handed out on printed sheets, with no indication of authorship. After careful and repeated readings the undergraduates wrote their comments, which Richards analysed. He claims (with obvious truth) that 'no higher standard of critical discernment can easily be found under our present cultural conditions'. The result is horrifying. Some of the best poems received the lowest marks; many readers failed to register what they were about; every felicity was ridiculed, and every absurdity praised, by large minorities and even majorities. From his analysis, Richards moves to a discussion of the chief difficulties of criticism, which is one of the clearest and sanest examples of critical writing in existence. Almost every problem of importance is dealt with. It is here that he sketches his famous theory of the four kinds of meaning—sense, feeling, tone and intention; he is excellent on rhythm ('a rhythm of the mental activity through which we apprehend not only the sound of the words but their sense and feeling'); he indicates the very source of poetic value in saying 'how very far ahead of us our words often are'; he uses, but does not abuse, the idea of stock responses. His remarks on Doctrinal Adhesion and criticism will be considered later. Perhaps the strongest impression left by this book is how little he deserves the charge, often made, and perhaps deserved by some of his other work, of being over-intellectual. For him, responding to poetry with one's whole being is the essential starting point of all criticism:

> *Critical* certainties, convictions as to the value, and kinds of value, of kinds of poetry, might safely and with advantage decay, provided there remained a firm sense of the importance of the critical act of choice, its difficulty, and the supreme exercise of all our faculties that it imposes.

If a group of Cambridge undergraduates would, as one feels fairly certain, fare better in a similar test today, it is hardly too much to say that this book is responsible.

William Empson has often called himself a disciple of Richards: partly in modesty, but also in candour. He is the author of three volumes of criticism whose brilliance has dazzled a generation. The first, *Seven Types of Ambiguity* is a hotch-potch of comments on odd bits of poetry, arranged in an unsatisfactory scheme which he hardly believes in himself, in which he searches restlessly for, and easily finds, concealed puns and complexities of meaning. *Some Versions of Pastoral* includes essays on Shakespeare, Marvell, Milton, Gay, Lewis Carroll and Proletarian Literature. The third and most, ambitious book, *The Structure of Complex Words* straddles literary criticism and linguistics; its main interest is the complexities of meaning and feeling contained in such words as 'honest', 'dog', 'sense' and 'fool', and 'equations' between these made by a particular use of the word. It includes an analysis of *Othello* which maintains that the play depends on a hidden pun on the word 'honest', a suggestion for improving dictionaries, a sketch of the history of unofficial belief in England, and a frighteningly cynical account of Shakespeare's aims in *Measure for Measure*.

Reading Empson is like struggling breathless after an accomplished mountaineer who climbs with elegant and alarming speed while

> *The increasing prospect tires out wandering eyes,*
> *Hills peep o'er hills, and Alps on Alps arise!*

But you never quite lose sight of him. He will take a sudden plunge into the abyss with some absurdity, but no scream comes up to your ears; did he not laugh as he fell past you ('Speculation on these lines is I suppose pretty useless. . . .')? And a moment later he is at your elbow, carefully placing your hand in a hold and wrapping your fingers round the comfortable rock. Perhaps after all we shall reach the top of the Alps, even of A£1 and Depreciative Pregnancy!

To decide about Empson's merits seems to need Coleridge's distinction between genius and judgement; or Pope's:

> *Some, to whom Heaven in wit has been profuse,*
> *Want as much more to turn it to its use;*
> *For wit and judgement often are at strife,*
> *Though meant each other's aid, like man and wife.*

The qualities are contrasted, but the term, 'wit', is the same; just as husband and wife, Empson himself points out, are not denied the same surname. This suggests that genius and judgement are not contrasting faculties but a matter of how you feel disposed to deploy rather similar abilities. It seems unfair, when you think about Empson, that so much intelligence should have been lavished on one man: not unfair on others, but unfair on him. No-one could have the judgement to turn all those ideas to relevance; lesser men will write the dictionary he suggests, prune and apply his theories.

Empson is a theoretical critic; his most brilliant analyses can be quite useless for evaluating a poem. Curiosity not judgement is the motive, and his question is less often What is this poem doing and is it good? than How is it doing it? This is admitted very frankly in the Preface to the second edition of the *Seven Types*, one of the best things he has written. 'The judgement indeed comes earlier or later than the process which I was trying to examine.' It seems fitting to end a discussion of Empson on an ambiguity, so I will point to the one we have in the word judgement. As used by Coleridge and (probably) Pope it does not suggest evaluation or aesthetic reaction; as used in this paragraph it does. Empson lacks both kinds of judgement (of course there are shining exceptions) and the two faults are not the same. Slipshod judgement (Pope's) can damage theoretical criticism, when he cannot resist the fidgets and prune his essay; and the tidiest discussion may shirk judgement, in the sense of value-judgement. Yet we do use the same word for both, and it cannot be wholly coincidence that the same critic is deficient in both. I commend the connexion to Mr. Empson himself.

We are now more or less into the realm of theoretical criticism proper. We move right inside with R. G. Collingwood's *Principles of Art*. If this marvellous book has a fault, it is that the practical consequences are not worked out in sufficient detail. Not that Collingwood was not interested in them: he claims in the preface that everything is meant to have 'a practical bearing, direct or indirect, upon the condition of art in England in 1937'. The argument of the book is that art is the expression of emotion and is a form of language. In the first part things which look like art (craft, magic) are distinguished from it. The second part elaborates a theory of imagination which draws on most of traditional philosophy and defiantly ignores most modern psychology, which Collingwood loathed. Only in the short third part does he discuss the artist and the community, and comment on the position of the arts today. His discussion of what it is to 'understand' a work of art is the finest I know; it enables one to sort what is true from what is false in Coleridge's over-quoted remark that poetry gives most pleasure when 'only generally and not perfectly understood'; and the illustration used, an analysis of Eliot's *Sweeney among the Nightingales* is a perfect piece of practical criticism. Perhaps it is worth remarking that the philosopher Collingwood seems to have appreciated Eliot when most of the professional critics were still resisting him.

The question of schools of criticism—approaches to literature that start from strong extra-literary presuppositions—belongs under the heading of theoretical rather than practical, for the reason already stated: that differences in presuppositions result in differences of evaluation with surprising rarity. When they seem to, it is often no more than a prejudice: predispositions will more frequently blind a critic to a poem than cause him to disapprove of an aim he perceives clearly. The two main sets of presuppositions we have—Marxism and Christianity—will make their most genuine appearance not in the judgement of actual poems, but in the elaborating of a view of what literature is for.

Marxism is so out of favour in Britain nowadays that to write about it at all may seem quaint. When it was sweeping all before it in the 30's the scrupulous intellect was that which queried its dogmas; today a proper impartiality might suggest a defence. It is true that any defence must shudder at the dreary incompetence of most Marxist critics, but they are not the first who have applied valuable principles without intelligence. Arnold Kettle shows a wiser sensibility in his two volumes on the English novel, but the much-praised Christopher Caudwell is heavy going: his account of Elizabethan drama makes one feel that not only would it be easy to write a better history of this subject, it would be easy to write a better Marxist history. This cannot be said of George Thomson, whose big book *Aeschylus and Athens*, and whose little book, *Marxism and Poetry*, take us as far as these theories can. What is really of value in the Marxist view of literature is the habits it encourages: the literary historian is the better for a sense of smell that keeps him aware of the social structure of an age; and the critic of contemporary writing for remembering that there are others in the community besides writers, critics and professors, and that other things being equal (alas how seldom they are!) the wider a book's appeal the better. The ferocious anti-Marxist may insist that there are other, less disreputable sources of these habits; though I doubt if any other is so effective.

If Marxism in England has become either archaic or diluted, almost the opposite is true of Christianity. Among intellectuals Christian belief is widespread and may be growing; yet our society is steadily un-Christian in so many of its assumptions. So although there is no 'school' of Christian critics as there was (and elsewhere still is) of Marxists, the problem of belief is probably the central problem of modern criticism, and it concerns Christians above all. In an age of varied and often incompatible beliefs we have developed a museum attitude to art, a historical catholicity of taste determined to enjoy the best of every age and clime. Naturally then the problem should present itself, how do we come to value a work of literature when we reject the beliefs it is built on? There is no doubt of the fact that we do this, but explanations have tended to be superficial or question-begging. The false and unworthy view of A. E. Housman, that what a poem says is of no importance as long as it is melodious and suggestive, is fortunately dying; for more serious suggestions we can turn to I. A. Richards (especially the early essay *Science and Poetry*), and T. S. Eliot. There seem to be two main explanations: that there are two kinds of belief, and that there are two kinds of truth. The first is the view of Richards: that emotional belief need not involve intellectual belief, and that though in the past the two have mingled, poetry now provides a way of achieving the former without its leaning on the latter. Richards' view has met with a great deal of resistance; he saluted *The Waste Land* for effecting 'a complete severance between poetry and all beliefs' and an obviously pained Eliot dissociated himself apologetically from this view. In the same work (*The Use of Poetry*) Eliot made his own suggestions on the matter. They come in the essay on Shelley; after attempting to account for his distaste for Shelley's poetry, he concludes:

When the doctrine, theory, belief, or "view of life" presented in a poem is one which the mind of the reader can accept as coherent, mature, and founded on the facts of experience, it interposes no obstacle to the reader's enjoyment, whether it be one that he accept or deny, approve or deprecate. When it is one which the reader rejects as childish or feeble, it may, for a reader of well-developed mind, set up an almost complete check.

Now coherence and fidelity to the facts of experience are tenable definitions of truth; and so the non-Christian reader 'accepts' *Paradise Lost* because its view of man, of temptation and of evil, seem to him in an important, if not in the only sense, true. To say this is merely the beginning of the argument, but it seems a more fruitful beginning than Richards'. There is a sort of aggressive scepticism about Richards' theory that makes it inconceivable to think of a Christian holding it; whereas Eliot is concerned for the undevout as well as the devout. Eliot does in fact carry the argument further, rather tentatively in the study of Dante, but with splendid assurance in the masterly *Shakespeare and the Stoicism of Seneca*.

Before leaving Eliot one must mention the two critical concepts to which he has given so much meaning, and which may not be unrelated to his Christianity: tradition, and impersonality. The concepts run through all his work, and are dealt with explicitly in *Tradition and the Individual Talent*, perhaps the most influential critical piece of the century. His view of the impersonality of great poetry is a theory (dare one say a truth?) of no less importance than Coleridge's account of the imagination, and perhaps the most important critical idea since then. 'Impersonal' is of course a term of blame in literary criticism: Richards complained that certain bad poems 'might well have been written by a committee', and George Orwell actually has the sentimental songs of 1984 composed by machines. To see that this use of the term is still valid, and that there is nonetheless another form of impersonality that is the mark of greatness, has now become the basic training of the critic. Perhaps this contribution alone places Eliot as the greatest of modern critics.

Behind Eliot stands the figure of T. E. Hulme, whose *Speculations* seems to anticipate many of his ideas and even phrases. Hulme arrived at a cool intellectual acceptance of religion ('It is not that I put up with the dogma for the sake of the sentiment, but that I may possibly swallow the sentiment for the sake of the dogma') by sitting in judgement on all human history: his criticism tries to be just as cool, and his favourite word of abuse is Romanticism. Hulme did not live to work out his brilliant and arrogant theories in detail, and it may not be possible now to decide if he was a great original genius, or merely had his ear close to the ground.

I come to the last section, which must be treated briefly: the historical critics. Here too there is a cleavage between practical and theoretical aims, and a close intermingling in fact. It is possible to study the literature of the past without making the assumption that it will be like ours or offer us what we ask from poetry. This is the historical approach; and just as it is now possible to analyse seventeenth-century politics without assuming that it was dominated by the passion for constitutional liberty so dear to the nineteenth-century historian, so it is possible to read seventeenth-century poetry in the light of what contemporaries expected it to be like. The literary critic I take to be concerned with the difference between good poems and bad; the literary historian with that between Augustan and Romantic poems. James Sutherland's *Preface to Eighteenth Century Poetry* is a perfect example of pure literary history: it is judicial, penetrating and sensitive, but disengaged; there is no plea for the poetry as valuable to us, merely an attempt to say what, at the time, it was like. The greatest of modern literary historians is C. S. Lewis. He has written, with very varying success, literary criticism, philosophy, Christian apologetics and Science Fiction; only in the field of literary history does he seem to me an assured master. Often in the same book the indifferent quality of the criticism seems amazing beside the brilliance with which the mind of a past age is recreated.

The historical is no doubt a perfectly proper approach to the literature of the past, but it does ignore the most important quality of literature, that it is not of an age but for all time; and to study it without bearing this in mind does seem like Hamlet without the Prince of Denmark. And so the trouble begins: literary historian and critic cannot leave each other alone. For in the first place the literary historian must be able to read poetry, sensitively, as poetry: this is what distinguishes him from a third figure, the scholar, whose task is to provide the means (text, biography and so on) for each of the others to go about his business. There is a constant assault by critics to suggest that these two are much the same and are doing something mechanical and not very important; so it is not surprising that the historian fights back by trying to teach the critic his business. He will point out that the meanings of the words in a poem may have changed, and every reader must know these; he may suggest that he ought to know more, to learn the Elizabethan World Picture from Professor Tillyard, the Chaucerian world from Livingstone Lowes, the Augustan poetic from Sutherland, before he can judge anything. Without doubt he will exaggerate the amount of background knowledge needed by the critic; in a brilliant analogy, Arnold Stein once pointed out that highly successful surgeons get along on a surprisingly poor knowledge of anatomy. But the historian does, sometimes, get his revenge: he catches the critic out in a palpable misreading, and mutual distrust grows even stronger. The classic controversy is that centred on the work of the American, Miss Rosamund Tuve. In *Elizabethan and Metaphysical Imagery*, and again in *A Reading of George Herbert*, she claimed that a number of modern critics, including Eliot and Empson, have misread the metaphysical poets. Eliot's excited discovery that Donne's use of language was especially congenial to the modern poet caused him to read a great deal into Donne that was not there; and the corrective to this is to look at contemporary poetic theory, and assume that a poem does what its author and reader asserted it was setting out to do. This in turn raises the issue (as Miss Tuve's opponents have not failed to point out) of the relation between intention and achievement. The reason why this is perhaps the most fruitful of modern controversies is not only that the issues are of importance, but also the formidable powers of Miss Tuve (no mere scholar she) and, above all, the central place that the metaphysicals hold in our view of English literature.

I cannot end by justifying, or even accounting for, modern English literary criticism; but perhaps one should end by pointing out that to many it does seem to need accounting for. Why this spate of criticism over the last 30 years, unprecedented in complexity, variety, or volume? Is it something new? It is hard to answer either Yes or No. In some senses it obviously is, and a glance at the seventeenth century shows us that much of the energy we spend on it was spent by them on biblical commentary and interpretation: there is much in common between the two skills. But insofar as one equates criticism with practical criticism, the critic being simply the more nearly perfect reader, one cannot maintain that it is new without claiming that we understand past literature better than those for whom it was intended— perhaps better than the author. 'Understand' is, to be sure, an ambiguous word here, but this is nonetheless the beginning of a very slippery slope. On the other hand, the attempt to say that modern criticism is not new has too hard a tussle with the facts. It usually rests on a claim that the standard of reading has declined, 'The New Criticism', writes Eric Bentley, 'does not tell us many things that would have been beyond Samuel Johnson's range. It tells us things that he would have considered too obvious to need saying.' This seems to me clearly nonsense. What is more tenable is the view that the seventeenth and eighteenth centuries read better than we, but were, in comparison, almost inarticulate about it. There is a slippery slope here too, leading to a defence of very sloppy reading, but it is less steep than the other. Whether the New Criticism is new turns out in fact to be not one question but several, and some can only be answered by guesswork and prejudice. New or old, necessary or redundant, we have got it, so we had better make the best of it. And the best is very good.

The Bloomsbury Tradition
in English Literary Criticism

PAUL BLOOMFIELD

MESSRS. BINDSCHAEDLER AND BURR no longer occupy their old premises at the western approaches of Gordon Square. Gone is the opaque window with the mysterious words in white paint, 'For Motor Companions', which roused somewhat ribald speculations in those about to set foot on hallowed ground. Bearing left, one would be recalled to order by the line of lofty plane-trees screening the row of houses where so many of the famous coterie were at home. They are elegant houses, in a heavy late Georgian way, with some Victorian additions tagging on at the south end. In a number of them was led a richly diversified and creative life, a life not quite *de Bohême* but unconventional.

The providers of Motor Companions have gone. The beautiful trees, however, stand their ground, and half a century after Leslie Stephen's daughters Vanessa and Virginia, pioneers of the Bloomsbury colony, chose to settle here, there are still two Strachey addresses in the square, and Lady Keynes is still at 46. When Maynard Keynes married the charming Russian dancer Lydia

Lopokova he was already a well-known public man. Nobody in the coterie moved in a larger social circle. With his official and academic connections, his intelligence, his feeling for the arts, his positive genius for finance (including investment), Keynes was a metropolitan among his friends. Scholars, writers, painters, psychologists, an economist and a ballerina—they made their mark severally and collectively.

Literary criticism was chiefly represented in Bloomsbury by Lytton Strachey and Virginia Woolf, who in the special circumstances were under obligations to George Moore, a Cambridge philosopher and critic of morals (most of the men had been at Cambridge); to Roger Fry, a critic of the plastic arts; to Clive Bell, a critic of painting and of the arts of living—in which he was reputed to be something of a connoisseur. This is not the whole story. If you have a set of talented people who know one another intimately and see one another constantly, you expect them to owe their friends more than the stimulus of particular theories. There is a ferment of ideas, which encourages each in his own bent, while at the same time mutual reactions and concessions bring into existence an ethos. So it was that the topographical name 'Bloomsbury' legitimately got a new significance.

Now in a memoir that Keynes wrote in 1938 he made what appears to be a rather surprising statement about the attitude of Bloomsbury in the early, formative days. 'We were not aware,' he said, 'that civilization was a thin and precarious crust erected by the will and personality of a very few, and only maintained by rules and conventions skilfully put across and guilefully maintained. We had no respect for traditional wisdom or the restraints of custom. We lacked reverence, as Lawrence observed . . . for everything and everybody.' What they *did* have, Keynes goes on to say, and he makes it responsible for a kind of superficiality which he alleges he shared with the others, was a complacent belief that human beings are by nature rational. They ignored 'certain powerful and valuable springs of feeling'. They were also too individualistic, not so much in overrating personal character as in underrating the power of those impulses which affect 'the order and pattern of life amongst communities, and the emotion they inspire.' The Freudian sun was about to come up: strange that in Bloomsbury it should have been so dark before dawn.

One has a suspicion that Keynes was saying too much. After all, young people with a disposition to reasonableness always examine traditional values before they accept them. If they are brilliantly clever their criticism will almost certainly be severe, partly because—in their impatience to be unshackled—they want to revenge themselves a little on the older generation, for *being* the older generation, and, if these were impressive, then for *being* impressive. The Bloomsbury ancestors were most impressive.

To go back for a moment to the memoir. 'As the years wore on towards 1914,' Keynes wrote, 'the falsity of our view of man's heart became, as it now seems to me, more obvious; and there was, too, some falling away from the original doctrine.' But the falsity of the view was already more obvious to some of the others—then. We can say, on the evidence, that they were picking up some anthropology and psychology more quickly than Keynes allowed. For the ball had opened, and Bloomsbury criticism had made its bow, with the appearance in 1912 of a small book in which the unreasonableness of exclusive rationality was acknowledged in the plainest words. Lytton Strachey's *Landmarks in French Literature* begins: 'When the French nation gradually came into existence among the ruins of the Roman civilization in Gaul, a new language was at the same time slowly evolving.' It is a model book, with not a flat sentence or trace of flagging zeal, and in it some of the features of the Bloomsbury tradition are already visible. Respect for tradition *tout court* is clearly one of them; we could not have a warmer celebration of gradual coming into existence and of slow evolving. And in Chapter Five, writing of Voltaire—his hero then and ever after—there is Strachey actually shaking his head over the arch-rationalist's immunity from those emotional states of mind 'which go to create the highest forms of poetry, music and art'; and he says 'this was certainly a great weakness in him—a great limitation of spirit'.

Five years later Strachey was famous—and infamous. *Eminent Victorians* had come out in 1918. The admirable life of Queen Victoria followed in 1921. For three later books of criticism it could be claimed that many of the essays in them were works of art. The last, *Characters and Commentaries*, was published in 1933, the year after Strachey's death at the early age of fifty-two.

To many of us who do not share Strachey's outlook his prose is a delight. The total effect of almost every one of his essays strikes me as characteristic, of a piece, and memorable. He is inspired by reason without being tainted by the recurrent heresy which consists in reason, that is to say reason's self-appointed champions, denying the existence of *what-is-given* when this apparently cannot be reconciled with its—reason's—own logic. He writes movingly of life and of death. But this is not what

Sir Herbert Read thinks. About a paragraph of Strachey's describing the death of Queen Victoria Read says: 'This is not an altogether bad piece of prose.' He admits that one notices 'a certain ironic affectation', but apart from this 'we are scarcely conscious of the kind of prose we are reading'. If this were true, then it was artful indeed of Sir Herbert to make the most of this particular passage, for it is generally agreed that the main objection to Strachey's prose is that its style is so catching, ironic affectation and all.

In a word, Sir Herbert disapproved of Bloomsbury. This comes out for instance in the essay he wrote on Roger Fry. Of the coterie he said: 'It turned with a shudder from the threatening advance of the proletarian "herd" '. It—how 'it' lumps them together!—did not attempt 'to reconcile its own traditions of good taste and refinement with the necessary economic foundations of a new order of society'. Now if nobody ever felt justified in seizing an opportunity offered by social or inherited advantages, and all eyes had to stay fixed on the unpredictable future till everybody at last was 'equal', 'good taste and refinement' might be long in coming. Besides, Sir Herbert is losing sight of the fact, that a very important—and well-assimilated—member of Bloomsbury, Leonard Woolf, was a Socialist. Sir Herbert has a formidable grasp, and disarming sympathies; and he is honest—has enough of the *mens conscia recti* not to be embarrassed when he changes his mind. But his appreciations somehow lack joy. His optimistic faith that 'the machine, mass-production and universal education' will bring forth good prose and fine poetry is honourable, and we should like to be able to hope he may prove right. But faith is not literary criticism.

When Thomas Hardy died, Virginia Woolf wrote in her beautiful essay on his novels: 'The peasants are the great sanctuary of sanity, the country the last stronghold of happiness.' And of popular art, perhaps. As things are going it looks as if only the spectacular arts, theatre and the ballet, stood a chance of being popular much longer. Literature? Nearly two hundred years ago Dr. Johnson was saying that 'people in general do not willingly read, if they can have anything else to amuse them.'

Meanwhile in 1925 Leonard and Virginia Woolf had published at the Hogarth Press—in those days in the basement of a house round the corner from Gordon Square—the latter's first *Common Reader*. It was dedicated to Lytton Strachey. 'The tower of Caister Castle still rises ninety feet into the air, and the arch still stands. . . .' These first words of the first essay in the book, on the Pastons and Chaucer, at once (*pace* Keynes again) betray a piety for the past. The Bloomsbury tradition, after all, is pregnant with respects and reverences. Even if it is not true—though like Matthew Arnold Mrs. Woolf believed it was—that 'it is impossible for the living to judge the work of the living' (or in other words that all criticism of new books is merely reviewing) . . . even if this is not true, most critics are chiefly kept busy by the past. If in their reassessments they show signs of disdainfully exposing, in a dead writer, what they would never have looked on as faults if they had been his contemporaries, then they are not in any Bloomsbury tradition.

Strachey wrote no novels, unless it is facetiously suggested that *Elizabeth and Essex* was one. Virginia Woolf wrote many, so we can congratulate ourselves that she found time for enough literary criticism to fill more than

the two *Common Readers*. These, with Strachey's biographical essays, could be our criteria for present purposes, and they are the most readable books of English
literary criticism since Pater. But I should put beside
them Aldous Huxley's *Texts and Pretexts*.

2

Like Strachey, Mrs. Woolf was the child of a conscientious agnostic. Her father, Sir Leslie Stephen, was
a pivotal Victorian figure; in early life he had for a time
been in Holy Orders. Bloomsbury was agnostic, and
Bloomsbury agnosticism had no place for even such
cautious faith as Arnold's in a power 'not ourselves, that
makes for righteousness'. This is a reason, though not
the only one, why contemporary Arnoldians are not in
the Bloomsbury tradition—any more than the *enfants
du siècle* at the antipodes from them.

By comparison with such ephemera Arnoldians are
rocks of ages. They have a *Weltanschauung*, a world outlook in the sense of philosophy of social life, the kind of
creative philosophy we particularly associate with the
great synthesis-making critic Matthew Arnold himself.
By his standards Bloomsbury had no *Weltanschauung*;
Bloomsbury's vicarious anxieties—and as a matter of
fact they were benevolent people—were not uttered with
the Arnoldian intonation at all. Strachey had an aloofness. He was no moralist. Coming though he did of a line
of colonial administrators, men ready to take the responsibility of ordering the lives of thousands or millions,
Strachey was a scholar, a man of taste, a clerk body and
soul. He was not going to bite off more than he could
chew. Virginia Woolf was against philosophical system-

166

atizing. In October 1932, when she was fifty, she wrote in her diary: 'It's so barren: so easy: giving advice on a system. The moral is, if you want to help, never system-atize—not till you're 70: and have been supple and sympathetic and creative, and tried out all your nerve and scopes.'

The Arnold tradition has been upheld in the last twenty-five years by the most eminent living English man of letters, Aldous Huxley. This is appropriate, for Mr. Huxley is Arnold's great-nephew. We have heard a good deal about the impossibility—'since Goethe' is often specified—of any man being a 'universal genius' any more. But we can be sure that even Goethe was not profoundly versed in *all* the sciences. Is the argument sup-posed to lead to the conclusion that because nobody can know everything, everybody in future must be resigned to being a specialist, and only a specialist, in however small a way? The Arnold tradition is to try to see things in just perspective even in these circumstances. But we must not forget that Arnold was a poet. And, to be fair, we must also bear in mind that Bloomsbury writing, critical writing included, was concerned with the values *in themselves* which Arnold in his systematic mood merely busied himself arranging in order.

Mr. Huxley, it need hardly be stressed, is a very learned man as well as an enterprising synthesis-maker, and when he criticizes he brings to the art a touch as delicate as it is energetic: he has the hand of a master. Take one of his short pieces, his essay on D. H. Lawrence. This does not remotely resemble the agitating and sensi-tive work of art Virginia Woolf might have produced— if she could have brought herself to write the memoir of a genius whose personality gave her such uncomfortable sensations. Nor is it like, say, Strachey on Voltaire and England, beautifully balanced, entertaining and acute as this is. But it is the expression of a masculine and vigorous talent. Mr. Huxley's manner suggests life at the growing point or a giant in his stride—a gentle giant so far as the difficult Lawrence is concerned.

T. S. Eliot, his Arnoldian sympathies and religious feeling still inhibited, might—with his early *Waste Land* verses—have seemed at least affiliated to Blooms-bury. By 1938 the poet Louis MacNeice, then about thirty, was writing shrewdly of him: 'With Eliot we meet a poet who has a world-view and is interested in the study of mankind. His world-view is defeatist, and he sees mankind through the glasses of a pedant, but he is at least civilized, synoptic, and—with allowance made for his pedantry—a realist. And for all his talk in his critical writings of impersonality, Eliot is a very personal poet.'

The MacNeice passage occurs in *Modern Poetry*, a book about modern poets, the author himself among them. Poets on poets: that had been the first English literary criticism. They made such good prose of it, that their essays would have called for criticism even if there had been no history, or, later, fiction, to require for prose the services of this ancillary art. Sir Philip Sidney with his endearing grace, Dryden with his flights of fancy, let it be clear at the outset that they had no intention of being academic, and certainly none of being boring. Criticism was something in its own right. The way things are said—style—has a bearing on what is said, just as manners have on what is done. The essential sub-stance of literature is wrapped in human personality, and art and criticism are processes of unravelling: 'the soul itself is truth', Yeats said.

Then what is it that the soul reveals about itself, or professes, when it speaks with the tongues of all whom it has 'inspired' since the day when Hesiod's shepherd was briefed by the Muses? It is undoubtedly part of a critic's business to try to find out. He is not likely to succeed unless he has certain personal endowments, or if he has no idea what he is looking for. Our affair here is less with the message than with the critic's powers of cognition and sense of responsibility.

3

'"To see the object as in itself it really is", has been justly said to be the aim of all true criticism whatever; and in aesthetic criticism the first step towards seeing one's object as it really is, is to know one's own impression as it really is. . . .' This is Pater speaking, and it follows from what he says that a good deal depends on the sensibility of whoever is receiving the impression.

The eminent Bloomsbury aesthetician, Roger Fry, while recognizing that unusual—and measurable, why not?—sensitivity was indispensable to a critic (of prose and poetry as well as of the visual arts), trusted to certain inherent qualities in the 'object' for keeping the critical balance dressed. They were the qualities peculiar to any art, the beauties not in the eye of the beholder, which give the art its power of evoking 'aesthetic emotion'. In prose and verse the objective element is presumably style.

The most deliberate literary stylist in Bloomsbury was David Garnett—not *ipso facto* the most careful writer. How far he was influenced by Fry I should not venture to guess, but he composed his remarkable books on an aesthetic principle. He suppressed the pervasive narrator, the intrusive moralist, the whisperer between the lines. He aimed at a kind of consistency by trying to let his stories tell themselves. D. H. Lawrence, who hated this impersonal manner, may have been thinking of Garnett, and of the early Joyce of *Dubliners*, when he described such writing (he did so in the preface of one of his Verga translations) as no less 'conceited' than wrong-headed.

What then were the objects on which Strachey and Mrs. Woolf relied for counterweighing *their* subjectivism, the lightning-conductors for their flashes of perception? Shall we find them being guided by Fry's theory or Garnett's practice (improbable, as he was a good deal their junior)? A picture should perhaps be pictorial, and a bronze should have bronziness; but need style be stylish? An immense amount of uninhibited, awkward and stilted writing—as in Dickens, Browning, Hardy—has added up to great literature. Let us hear Pater again. He says: 'What is important is not that the critic should possess a correct abstract definition of beauty for the intellect, but a certain kind of temperament, the power of being deeply moved by the presence of beautiful objects.'

Though at first it sounds as if the question were being begged—sensibility is all—we are really a little further on. For the beginning of Pater's sentence contains the important admission that a general aesthetic principle applicable to *whatever carries conviction* has never been discovered, and is never likely to be. The next writer of genius who comes along carrying conviction will also bring with him a licence to break what rules he feels he must. It happens that David Garnett was brilliantly successful. Would even his warmest admirer have expected everyone in future to try to write in the same way? Mrs. Woolf, for one, was not doing so, nor did she do so later. In short, to discover the controls of Strachey's and Mrs. Woolf's sensibilities—and allowing for the great differences between them—we have to look to no 'abstract definition' of anything, but to the conditions which fostered the Bloomsbury ethos. And the only reasonable method of judging whether N or M is in the Bloomsbury tradition is to understand that ethos and to consider to what extent N or M shares it.

Our fundamental axiom must be that the members of the Bloomsbury coterie sprang almost one and all from the great effective bourgeoisie of the last century, England's serious-minded and powerful liberalizing professional middle class. Many Stephens and their blood relations had been eminent public servants; the Stracheys had distinguished themselves particularly in India. The Garnetts showed hereditary ability too, and Roger Fry belonged to the philanthropic Quaker cousinhood into which Elizabeth Gurney had married—Mrs. Fry the prison reformer, that is to say. It is brash if we speak of the 'bourgeois virtues' to include ironically what we really think of as bourgeois vices, for instance immoderate conventionality. Legalism and *mesquinerie* or pettiness are bourgeois failings, and so is hypocrisy over sex; but not all bourgeois have had these at any time. The educated middle class are the middle way people, and their middlingness, like their regularity and habits of hard work, is a virtue born perhaps of necessity, but none the less a virtue: the same necessity would have broken ancestors of less tough fibre and scattered their seed to the winds. If history is going to be a success it will be by civilization becoming stabilized on an upper-middle-class level.

In past centuries it did not enter literate people's

heads to doubt that there was such a thing as excellence. Though there have always been the familiar jealousies and backscratchings, better and worse in literary performance were assumed to be referable to 'eternal standards'. There was no *class* jealousy: if the poor scholar or poet excelled, he did so according to those standards and was welcome to his laurels. As late as the eighteenth century William Blake, who was not a socialite, declared us all contemporaries *vis-à-vis* excellence. 'The ages are all equal,' he said, 'but genius is always above the age.' With the qualifications one has to make if one knows some history Hazlitt believed the same, though he was a radical: so did Pater, who was not; so did Strachey and Mrs. Woolf congruously with their upper-middle-class Bloomsbury ethos.

What are we to think of the great modern heresy, concomitant of proletarian revolution, that all art must be judged by its immediate universal acceptability? If no bounds were set to human faculty, if advances in politics, thought and art could occur *pari passu*, there might perhaps be something in it. But as things are and human nature being what it is, that is to say finite except in relation to the transcendental, it is of the greatest importance that we should keep our freedom to be envious, to admire, and—if we can—to excel. Addressing recriminations to the past for not being spiritually After Marx is terribly unrealistic, as well as rather ignoble.

Keynes has told us that he became aware that 'civilization was a thin and precarious crust erected by the will and personality of a very few'; how long had it been before the eyes of the rest of the coterie were opened? Freud's essay on *The Disillusionment of War*—about the thinness and precariousness of that crust—was written in 1915, and must have reached Lytton Strachey's psychologist brother James at the earliest possible moment. In her second novel, *Night and Day* (1919) Mrs. Woolf showed she knew something about the links of blood and tradition which hold civilization together. The coterie's reaction against unsympathetic father-figures was nothing like as important as their sense that it was *only congruous* to be identified with traditions of intellectual integrity and respect for talent. In relation to society they were good upper-middle-class; and though not Christians they were After-Christians; and they had no use for the *pari passu* heresy.

A reaction against the parents there was, of course. Though there may be, and I believe there is, a Oneness underlying the appearance of multiplicity, it is vain for determinism to insist on a kind of consolidated motive in everything that has motion. An artistic coterie, like a Communist Party, segregates itself and takes a line. Segregated impulses and conflicts are the bricks of the structure that may or may not have been blue-printed before the beginning of years. Bloomsbury amended the parental complex of congruities and was Bloomsbury, something now fairly far removed from the Clapham of the Quaker and Evangelical ancestors. Some of the differences were a matter of a shifting of emphasis only.

At any rate there were at least these three principles underlying Bloomsbury literary criticism: that personality and merit must be respected, that 'in all ages there have been some excellent workmen and some excellent work done' (Pater yet again), and that it is a religious duty to preserve the freedom of thought to be sceptical. To give the *Zeitgeist* priority over these assumptions would have seemed to the coterie at best a confession of immaturity, at worst callowness or a mark of inferior natural endowments. The spirit of the age can be a traitor. There is no inevitable progress, by dialectical materialist or other kinds of eventfulness, and since man refuses to stay still—usually preferring almost any commotion to serenity—he may as likely as not be found moving in the wrong direction.

But the *Zeit* has to have a *Geist*, it cannot help itself. The instability of the age is expressed, not only reflected, in much contemporary criticism which hardly allows us to locate the critic's position. What a merit it is in V. S. Pritchett that he, claiming so little ground for his own, should be able to offer us such confident, such glittering appreciations of literature. . . . I am sure 'glittering' came to me because his feat reminds me of Sergeant Troy's famous display in 'the hollow amid the ferns'. A foothold and his broadsword were all the Sergeant needed. Mr. Pritchett's style dazzles, and it is sometimes hard to remember the mould sculptured by his cuts and thrusts. As soon as the performance is repeated we are amazed once again.

Half a generation younger than Mr. Pritchett, Philip Toynbee in his novels has shown the *avant-garde* touch. The French idiom denotes a nuance of cultural liveliness not very often observed over here. Mr. Toynbee's criticism is sensitive to movements on the 'thin crust of civilization' or below it. But he is no longer keeping his ear too zealously close to the ground. His writing is admirably articulate. He is in the tradition; and unless his skill in avoiding dullness and clichés and the stilted or too-abstract phrase is to be regarded as his own patent, then to this extent he is in the *Bloomsbury* tradition.

4

The criticism most people in England read is contained in newspaper reviews. About the time when Oliver Goldsmith was struggling for a livelihood, in the middle of the eighteenth century, the increase of a literate public called reviewers into existence alongside of the critics; about a quarter of the way through the twentieth the decrease of literary magazines led to a certain confounding of the two functions.

Virginia Woolf thought it was a dreadful situation, and said so in a sixpenny Hogarth Pamphlet. To this Leonard Woolf added a note defending reviewers, but insisting as she did that reviewing, 'is quite distinct from literary criticism'. On the next page he writes: 'Literary magazines have failed. . . .' This is nearly true. The patient direction of such magazines by John Lehmann, Cyril Connolly and Stephen Spender for many years now has required exceptional measures—measures no doubt commercially profane. Mr. Woolf goes on: 'The modern reading public is not interested in literary criticism, and you cannot sell it to them.'

Exactly. Therefore the critics who have to write to live write reviews, but as they feel it would destroy them to behave as if their whole duty was—as Mr. Woolf maintained—'to give the reader a description of a book and an estimate of its quality', they do something more. They assert their personalities and mix in some criticism, and a strange brew the more inept ones make of it. And yet this is a sound principle, and it is the one that Mrs. Woolf and Lytton Strachey would obey if they were living now and were obliged to review new books. A critical review cannot be expected, like a good essay, simply to give pleasure: it might have to give pain— though not to the reader. But it must at least approximate to an essay in its arguments and presentation 'being so fused' as not to rend 'the surface of the texture'. It is true, as Mrs. Woolf also said, that 'beauty and courage are dangerous spirits to bottle in a column and a half'. But under duress that is what she would have tried to do; her personality—not her ego—would have taken charge. Personality fuses, the ego usually causes disintegration. The Bloomsbury tradition in literary criticism is a matter of learning, argument, bias and judgement 'being so fused by the magic of writing', being so transmuted by personality, that the final product, even when the scale is miniature, is an end in itself. (Mr. Woolf's formula will however do—indeed it is ethically speaking obligatory—when there is only *half* a column or less for the notice of a new book.)

The line between personality and ego is not always easy to draw, and it cannot of course be taken for granted that the use of the first person singular is a mark of egoism. In his appendix to the Hogarth pamphlet on reviewing Mr. Woolf actually ignores a compromise of which his wife speaks, the system of 'hedging' confessed to by Sir Harold Nicolson. 'I address myself to the authors of the books which I review; I want to tell them why I either like or dislike their work; and I trust that from such a dialogue the ordinary reader will derive some information.' So much, as Mrs. Woolf says, for any chance of criticism by reviewers being concerned with the 'eternal standards'! But she appreciates Sir Harold's 'honesty', and of course his qualifications as a reviewer-critic—to say nothing of his original works.

The question then is, in whose keeping are those
eternal standards for which Bloomsbury was solicitous?
University dons are certainly under an obligation to do
something about them. This raises the problem of con-
gruousness again. Dons are not expected to react too com-
promisingly to their likes and dislikes, and they would
mostly not have become dons if their make-up had included a strong dose of the existential alcohol. Many of
them show signs of being irked by their condition and
what is congruous with it. They are rather in the position
of judges, who, whether they like it or not, have to
administer not Justice but the law; but certainly worse
would befall if judges and dons failed in their duty. And
besides, some first-rate critics have been dons. Pater himself was a don, and so is his own latest critic, Lord David
Cecil. Bloomsbury, in Sir Herbert Read's words, 'was
nourished if not born, at Cambridge'. Are Cambridge
dons, Cambridge critics, Bloomsbury any more? Does
Bloomsbury linger on at King's? To hear Mr. Rylands
talking about Shakespeare on the wireless with the
authenticity of intelligent conversation suggests that the
answer is yes; but then Mr. Rylands was *of* Bloomsbury.
Mr. Annan, the able biographer of Leslie Stephen, of the
same college, sounds a different note—has a different
scale of priorities: there is business to be despatched. Mr.
Annan is a historian immune from Strachey's influence.

Oxford? Not long ago an Oxford don spoke acidly of
pre-war Balliol as that 'little Cambridge-in-Oxford'.
The College of Arnold and Palgrave and some others, of
whom presently, can take it. Let us turn to an Oxford
woman, Miss Wedgwood, who is not a don, but as a
historian impeccable, I imagine, from an academic point
of view. Her *Seventeenth Century English Literature*

(which appeared in the Home University series nearly forty years after Strachey's little book on French literature) is an outstanding essay in literary criticism. One would say she had read Virginia Woolf with much pleasure, and had not needed to learn from Strachey's mistakes. She is too eclectic to have the Bloomsbury people's idiosyncrasies imputed to her, but she comes of rather the same kind of distinguished *grand bourgeois* stock that they did, the kind it would take more than a college of logical positivists to mock from their humanist humour.

Naturally any interesting culture is bound to have its lively and its dour secessionists. Eton would in the usual way have offered Cyril Connolly and George Orwell the Bible with one hand and the Greek and Latin Classics with the other. Many a 'good'—many a *true*—Christian has emerged from our famous schools unaware of any difficulty in reconciling the two systems. Mr. Connolly chose Paganism. The late George Orwell rejected both, because neither seemed to him to offer an honest man a way of life congruous with his obligations to others. He wanted none of the consolations of the middle class ethos. All this naturally affected such criticism as he wrote. What he says about Dickens, for instance—a subject, by the way, that did not tempt Strachey or Mrs. Woolf—is worth reading. Not only had Nazism, war and cold war made detachment impossible for many writers—it had made it impossible for them in retrospect: Dickens himself was not *engagé* enough for Orwell. The old humanitarianism, like the old liberalism, had been reassessed and found hopelessly wanting in urgency. One voice, too rarely heard, which has continued to speak calmly in the unregenerately civilian, reflective accents of Bloomsbury, and with a kindliness of its own, even in wartime, is that of E. M. Forster, who was actually Bloomsbury-out-of-Clapham.

Mr. Connolly's antecedents we know from his own account of them. 'My previous incarnations: a melon, a lobster, a lemur, a bottle of wine, Aristippus. Periods when I lived: the Augustan age in Rome, then in Paris and London from 1660 to 1740, and lastly from 1770 to 1850.' But not, during this last phase, in Clapham among the Evangelicals. It is true that the list of 'friends' he claims among writers of the past includes many who were Strachey's friends too—the seventeenth- and eighteenth-century French paragons of elegant scepticism, and Hume and Walpole; it is true, without being significant. This invigorating and more manic than depressive pessimist sees the future greyer than Bloomsbury did. 'One day these huge crowds' (of the 'lovable' English masses) 'will have to seize power because there will be nothing else for them to do, and yet they neither demand power nor are ready to make use of it; they will learn only to be bored in a new way.'

Nowadays Mr. Connolly is the colleague on the *Sunday Times* of Raymond Mortimer, some of whose admirable critical essays were published by the Hogarth Press in 1942. (Is it not high time there was a successor to *Channel Packet?*) Some years ago Mr. Mortimer publicly repudiated his University. He explained himself, saying his affinities were all with Cambridge—and Bloomsbury. But he is an Oxford man; indeed he is a Balliol man. This is not the place to enquire how it happens that so many of our literary critics in the last hundred years—Arnold and Palgrave among them, as I have already said, and the Arnoldian Aldous Huxley—should have been Balliol men. Perhaps it is a coincidence. Cyril Connolly would have scintillated if he had been neither at Oxford nor Cambridge. But he was at Balliol too.

And so was Sir Harold Nicolson. Sir Harold, a most civilized writer, stands in the eyes of many readers for the type of mundane, well-informed, eloquent reviewer-critic, and in him they feel they get the best of both worlds, the sense of Oxford and the sensibility of Cambridge-in-Bloomsbury; his—and his wife's—Bloomsbury affinities and friendships are well known. Has he always been able to keep up those fruitful dialogues with the authors he reviews? Not Bloomsbury, not even Balliol has been able to solve the problem of being, at short notice, fair as well as 'personal with passion' (which is only too easy) about the living—in the space of between six hundred and sixteen hundred words. What critic since Macaulay has not sighed with relief at the opportunity of letting himself go about old books and authors when new authors have written new books on them?

Unfortunately the longer a list of the foregoing kind becomes the more invidious it is apt to be. But this consideration is not going to deter me from mentioning two people who eminently share the Bloomsbury concern for the decencies of criticism. The one is an independent, whose patient selflessness cannot have escaped the notice of anyone else with the same preoccupation: Edwin Muir—neither Oxford nor Cambridge, Balliol nor Bloomsbury, once a bank-clerk in Glasgow. And last, and how far from least, always conscientious to a fault, both the writer's—especially the novelist's—and the reader's friend (and a Balliol man), now perhaps forgotten as a reviewer but, by a freak of poetic justice, in the running for immortality as a novelist: L. P. Hartley.

It is all very well, though, to write as if the Bloomsbury

and other traditions between them have been giving
general satisfaction. This is not what the most intelligent
critics of thirty-five and under think of them. They are
by no means pleased even with some of the critics of
whom an older man speaks well out of grateful habits
which, he may be allowed to believe, were justified when
he was forming them. The situation is bad, and deteri-
orating. When Francis Birrell, whose early death was a
sad loss to the Bloomsbury tradition, wrote that 'the
intellectual journalist'—that is the reviewer-critic—is
with a few exceptions 'probably paid less money for
more work than any other bourgeois in England', conditions were actually less depressing than they are now.
Today the same kind of person does less work and is in a
greater hurry to rush off and sell his review copies at half
price. What is happening much too often is that if you
know something about the subject of a new serious book
you will be outraged by the foolish and superficial treatment it gets from reviewers writing in what are supposed
to be reputable papers. As for the public, who, as we
know from Dr. Johnson, Leonard Woolf and our own
observation, prefer all other entertainment to any reading except the lightest, they are now served by mighty
and indefatigable corporations flush with the public's own
or the advertisers' money, and directed by directors more
highly paid than the Archbishop of Canterbury.

Civilization is indeed 'a thin and precarious crust'.
It takes all sorts, and the patient practice of difficult
virtues, to create civilization, and violence could quickly
destroy it. To civilization Strachey and Mrs. Woolf made
distinguished contributions—congruous with other parts
of that whole, not only with a coterie spirit. They were
sensitive to impressions of individual personality. Strachey

was moved to irony by how people behaved to one another rather than by how fate behaved to them. Like him, in a manner all her own, Mrs. Woolf used words with care and judgement; she did so even when she was trying to tell us something almost incommunicable, as in her poetical vein she often did try. The art of sounding a personal note is, I think, in a dangerously depersonalized world, what it is most rewarding to study in their essays. It would hardly be that unless the consistently human touch, the refusal to treat people as their real selves when they are dressed up, or posing, or preaching, or justifying the means by the end, were so 'fused by the magic of writing' as to leave the matter purged of triviality. Such writing, such intelligence, such impressionableness, are rare at any time, and only too often conspicuous by their absence.

Historical Writing

C. V. WEDGWOOD

THE BUSINESS OF the historian is to communicate intelligible information about the past as clearly and accurately as he can. Historical writing therefore allows of less innovation and experiment than the novel, or poetry or drama. Though the historian may develop a highly personal style, the major changes in historical manner come more slowly than to other and freer forms of literature. Historical writing none the less reflects the epoch in which it is produced. Gibbon's high polish and cool humour belong to the eighteenth century, Carlyle's exclamatory vehemence to the mid-nineteenth, and Sir Lewis Namier's analytical precision is as much a product of the twentieth century as the impetuosity of Mr. A. L. Rowse. But the historian's style, however highly wrought, however personal, is held within the rigid limits imposed by his essential task—that of conveying what he believes to be accurate information as intelligibly as he can.

This historian may of course have other ideas as well as that of instructing in history. He may preach sermons, draw morals, or indicate political lessons; he may create an atmosphere in which to place his facts, or hint at underlying subtleties in the situation he is describing.

183

If he is an artist and a man of sensibility as well as a scholar he may so elaborate and select his language as to convey to the reader innumerable over and undertones to his theme. But all this must be in addition to the straightforward task of conveying information. If he fails in that, he fails altogether. For this reason the bolder and more ingenious experiments which constantly revitalize other branches of literature are forbidden to him.

Poets, novelists, dramatists can risk initial misunderstanding from the general public because they can always count on a minority who are aware of the necessity and value of experimental writing. A few will always be ready to grapple with the unfamiliar, even with the apparently incomprehensible, in the belief that a revelation may come and in the knowledge that without experiment and change in literature no new revelation can ever come. But few, if any, readers of history come to it looking primarily for something new and exciting in literature. The reader of history may be sensitive and imaginative in his appreciation of style; he may at other times be a patient and willing explorer of the difficult, the unfamiliar and the new in literature. But when he takes up a history book it is because he wants to discover or to re-call facts and ideas about the past. He may like the facts and ideas the better for being presented with elegance and form, even with a certain originality of phrase. But he will not go on with the book at all if he is left in any doubt as to what it all means. In this respect, and in this alone, a work of history is closer to a scientific treatise or a manual of engineering than to other forms of literature.

The literary imagination of the historian is curbed twice over—by his subject matter and by the attitude of his readers towards it. But if he is less free to experiment than are writers of other kinds he is wonderfully free in his choice of material. If there are necessarily fewer highly original minds among historians than among poets or novelists, there is a wider variety of writers. History covers the entire range of human activity and attracts practitioners of widely different kinds. History can be studied in vast perspectives of time and place or it can be examined under the microscope. Professor Arnold Toynbee's *Study of History* bestrides four thousand years and the entire globe. Sir Lewis Namier's *Structure of Politics* concentrates on one year, one problem and one country. An enquiry into the cultivation of root crops is one kind of history, a stirring account of the Peninsular War is another. There is no rule, although there may be a dominating fashion, to decree that one approach to history is better than another. The French Revolution can be treated as a violent human drama or reduced to the impersonality of economic analysis. The political correspondence of a prime minister or the milliner's bills of a grocer's wife, the impersonal entries of the customs house books, the public proclamation or the private diary are equally legitimate material for the historian. The rivalries of dynasties, the uprisings of peoples, the clash of interests in Court or Parliament, or round the parish pump, the greatest and the least, the most evidently important and the most apparently trivial, are all proper subjects for the historian's attention. History can be political, military, social, economic, legal, administrative, scientific, or philosophic. It can be presented as impersonally as an invoice or as vehemently as an election speech.

The study of history—which ultimately implies the

writing of history—thus attracts almost every kind of
temperament. This may be one reason why historians
seem to be subject not only to the personal rivalries which
are common to all writers, but to disagreements about
the approach to their subjects which can become extraordinarily bitter. Historians, more rapidly than other
writers, will outlaw works which do not meet with their
approval, declaring roundly that they are 'not history',
or, only a little less finally, 'not what *I* call history'.
Partly of course this is a problem of definition. A novelist
can say of another that he writes bad novels, or trivial
novels, or pretentious novels, but because there is a more
or less recognizable form called 'the novel' he cannot
say 'Blank doesn't write novels', with the superior scorn
with which the historian is sometimes heard to say
'Blank doesn't write history'. History—*written* history
—is a vaguer conception altogether and can be stretched
to cover at the one end works of conscious literary form
and high imaginative insight, and at the other the dryest
compilations of statistics. It is not therefore surprising
that practitioners of such very different kinds sometimes
find it difficult to accept each others claims. Though no-
one would advocate too casual an attitude to the standards
of scholarship, this excessive narrowness can be dangerous;
it is both possible and desirable that the cause of historical
knowledge should be served in as many different ways as
possible.

Changes in historical writing arise very largely from
changes in the character of the material with which the
historian is confronted. The major change in English
historical writing between Macaulay and Maitland arose
from the unprecedented increase in the amount of
material available; increased evidence enlarged the scope

of historical enquiry and so altered the whole technique and outlook of the historian. The decay of literary history and the rise of 'scientific' history was the inevitable response to the opening up of archives and the widening —and still widening—flood of evidence which the historian had to handle.

The overwhelming increase in the material, especially for the later periods of history, has in the present century given rise to the development of team work and co-operative history. Certain subjects and certain periods— the history of the last war, and the history of Parliament are two cases in point—can only be dealt with by a group of historians who can later pool and consider the results of research that no solitary enquirer could possibly undertake.

Some contend that the whole future of scholarly history lies in this direction. Collective history of this kind demands at once great and patient scholarship and considerable self-abnegation on the part of the scholars concerned. Those of us on the other hand who still feel that there is a future for history which combines literature and scholarship and for books which bear the imprint of a single mind admit the necessity for co-operative history in certain fields while often regretting that some of our most gifted and original historians have become so deeply involved. Sir Keith Hancock has been organizing the history of the war, Sir Llewelyn Woodward editing the monumental volumes of the British Diplomatic Documents. Both these undertakings are of the greatest value, but it is to be hoped that the insight, skill and personal distinction of both these historians—each in his own right as good a writer as he is a scholar—will ultimately be revealed again in independent work.

In the actual *writing* of history, the changes in this century, and more especially in the last generation have arisen from a process, half open, half tacit, of challenge and counter challenge. The effect of 'scientific' history on English historical style was deplorable. A few distinguished exceptions stand out; Frederick Maitland's masterly prose for instance. But in general the 'scientific' approach to history went with the rejection of the entire literary tradition of English historical writing. It became the fashion among scholars to assume that readable history was necessarily bad history, and the high priests of history as a science 'denounced from the altar any of the profession, alive or dead, who had had dealings with literature'. Against this view the young George Trevelyan uttered a memorable protest. The effect of this was twofold. He himself set an example in combining literary distinction with sound scholarship which has been followed by others both inside and outside the academic world.

Apart from the growth and flourishing of the renewed school of literary history of which he is the founder and still the greatest exponent, his challenge has had a secondary and indirect influence on the supporters of the more austere view of historical scholarship. The idea that the historian should have no dealings whatever with literature has almost wholly vanished; on the contrary the value of the study of literature and the importance of a clear and disciplined style is now generally emphasized in the universities. What is frowned on is *popularity*, the desire to communicate subtle and obscure historical discoveries to a large public. Much historical research which still needs to be done is not of a kind that can, by any exercise of literary talent or stretch of imagination, be made interesting to the many. Much really new and valuable work can, in the nature of things, only appeal to the few and only be made immediately comprehensible to those—fewer still—who are already well-informed on the background and nature of the problems discussed. (The same is of course true of research in the pure sciences, but there the additional question of literary quality has never arisen.) It is obvious that a book about Mary Queen of Scots or the American Civil War or the Industrial Revolution will have an immediate interest to a great number of people whether or not it contains anything new either of interpretation or information. But a study of the administration of a mediaeval monastic estate is of much more limited interest, and an enquiry into the earliest forms of writs of impeachment under Richard II may be comprehensible only to a small band of scholars.

Scholars who devote themselves to these more detailed enquiries quite rightly regard the wooing of the public as something entirely outside their sphere. But this does not prevent many of them from writing not only with firmness and clarity but sometimes with a sense of structure and a distinction of vocabulary which would—if their work were better known to non-historians—put them high among modern prose writers. Comparison of the articles and reviews in the *English Historical Review* in the early years of this century with those of to-day gives proof of the way in which the purely scholarly historians have tacitly accepted the importance of style. In the United States for instance, the aggressively anti-literary influence of the Germanic school of scholarship is still far more prevalent than it is here.

The antagonism between schools of thought in history

today is not so strong as it once was between the writer of history as literature, and the writer of history as scholarship. It is basically between the scholar and the popular historian. It is only fair to add that, bitter as these arguments sometimes are, a great number of historians, both literary and scholarly, are not concerned in them but are willing to accept that there is not only room for both, but a necessity for the existence of both within the profession.

The bitterness of the quarrel, when it does arise, and the interchange of sneers and denunciations which sometimes breaks out in the correspondence columns of the literary papers is partly the result of a contradiction in temperament, not only between two different historians but within the single mind of each. The desire to find out and the desire to communicate are totally different things. There is, in almost all who devote themselves to the study of history, a proportion of both qualities. At the extreme end of the scale, on one side, is the scholar who only desires to find out and who finds it almost impossible, when he has finished his quest, to communicate the result. It is saddening to think how much historical enquiry has gone for nothing because of a temperamental failing which sometimes goes with the most penetrating and patient minds. At the other end of the scale is the man whose desire to communicate overmasters him even when he has remarkably little to say. If the desire to communicate very strongly outbalances the desire to find out, the potential historian may degenerate fairly rapidly into a mere book-maker, working to a quick formula and using—or as the more sour in the profession would say—abusing historical themes. But if the desire to communicate is too feeble, then the promising young man who wrote a much admired monograph in his twenties, may turn into the distinguished, infertile scholar who every ten years or so contributes an article to a learned journal, and in the intervening time demolishes in the reviewing columns, with a knowledge that cannot be faulted, the works of anyone bold enough to trespass into his field of research. His own *magnum opus*, as he himself and everyone else gradually comes to accept, will never be written at all.

Consciously or unconsciously the too communicative historian knows where his weakness lies; consciously or unconsciously the silent scholar may envy the open facility of the other. Almost certainly both are a little at war with themselves. Historians are not as a rule an introspective race. They are more given to writing on the meaning and uses of history, than to examining the occupational diseases of the profession or investigating the subtler processes of composition in their own minds. This, on the whole, is just as well, but if a little more attention were sometimes given to the temperamental, as well as to the technical, problems of the craft there might be fewer false starts and less unfulfilled promise in the profession.

It cannot however be said that we are suffering from any shortage of historians, even of good historians, in England at the present time. Both popular history, literary history and scholarship are well served. Even if that were not so the decade since the war has seen the publication of one of those rare classics of history of which, in English literature, Clarendon's *Great Rebellion* has hitherto been the outstanding example. Sir Winston Churchill's *History of the Second World War* is an addition to historical literature of the same nature and magnitude. It is unusual for a statesman of outstanding gifts who has had the guidance of public affairs during a world crisis to possess also the literary skill to re-tell the story as a work of literature. Sir Winston has this and something more: he has a sure sense of historical perspective and a deep feeling for the value of the past and its relation to the present. This was shown in his life of Marlborough twenty years ago, perhaps still more in the eloquent *History of the English-Speaking Peoples* with which he has crowned his literary career. This quality combined with a massive and deliberate sense of form, and an artist's eye for detail, give shape and vigour to the most remarkable work of contemporary history of our time.

In the decade since the war Arnold Toynbee has completed his *Study of History*, a work as majestic in conception as it is impressive in the magnitude of its scope. There have been important works of sustained scholarship and literary skill—Steven Runciman's Crusades, Sir John Neale's books on the Parliaments of Queen Elizabeth, A. L. Rowse's first two volumes on the Elizabethan Age. Sir Arthur Bryant after completing his series on the Napoleonic Wars with his sparkling study of Regency England, has turned to what promises to be his crowning achievement, a general history of England.

In the field of mediaeval learning Sir Maurice Powicke has given us the fruit of a lifetime of work in the thirteenth century in *The Lord Edward*. Professor Sayles with quiet persistence and deep learning attacks the still dominant theories of Bishop Stubbs in mediaeval history, and in his *Mediaeval Foundations* set forth the development of a civilization with as much insight as style. D. M. Stenton's *English Society in the Early Middle*

Ages is another post-war triumph in a region of history not usually popular with the common reader. The admirable short book on *Prehistoric England* by Christopher and Jacquetta Hawkes proved that even the remotest and least documented ages can be made interesting to a wide public if learning is presented with imagination and grace. Professor V. Gordon Childe's *What Happened in History* must also, by its persuasive qualities have extended the time perspective of the ordinary reader.

All these books made their appearance in the bright blue livery of the Pelican edition, a fact which clearly indicates one of the most significant developments of the last generation, the coalescence and final triumph of two parallel ideas. While G. M. Trevelyan was crusading for a return to literary history which would be read by all educated men, he also complained that the general public were being frightened off the study of a subject from which they had much to learn. A growing literate public needed books that would assuage its thirst for knowledge in a manner that the average reader could understand, and at a price that the ordinary man could pay. The influence of another historian of the Trevelyan generation was thrown strongly on to the same side, and the Home University Library under the auspices of H. A. L. Fisher came into being. But the public increased rapidly during and immediately after the First World War, still more during the Second World War. This latter increase was thought by many to be merely temporary, the result of the lack of counter attractions, and the very scarcity of books which gave them an added charm. Ten years after the war it is clear that, in spite of rival demands on public attention, from the Third Programme to Television, a part of the new public has been retained. The demand for serious books is larger now than it was in 1939.

In the years between the wars the supply of history for the new and growing public did not, in spite of the Home University Library and its very considerable achievement, quite meet the demand. 'It was most unfortunate', wrote Professor C. H. Williams in 1938, 'that just when the historian was most in demand he was least in evidence. The result was inescapable. It was Mr. H. G. Wells'. The public could have done worse. The products of a vigorous and original mind are always stimulating to thought, even if Mr. Wells's historical knowledge was not quite equal to the ambitious and generous idea that he conceived in his history of the World. All the same, the diminishing difference between demand and response in the twenties and in the later forties shows how far things had altered. The public after the First World War got Mr. H. G. Wells. After the Second World War they got the learned specialists and first-class scholars bending their talents to a paper back edition. There are two things of great significance in this development, that an enterprising publisher should be prepared to present original works of learning in this form, and that scholars of reputation, depth and original-ity should be ready and should be able to co-operate.

It has been recognized in practice, if not yet quite universally in theory, that there is no essential anti-pathy between historical scholarship and literature. Further, that while certain subjects can never in the nature of things lend themselves to 'popularization', other subjects can and do; that the scholar and the popularizer can on occasion even be the same person. Only a small and purist group of scholars would now probably deny this. In the last years controversy in history is less often technical than, in essence, political. The arguments whose repercussions reach the ears of the general public are almost all of this kind, and their reality as well as their heat is generated by their open or tacit association with modern political controversy. The din of argument which arises round the economic interpretation of the English seventeenth century or the rights and wrongs of the Industrial Revolution is in essence the din made by irreconcilable modern factions, political and economic: Socialist against Conservative, Planner against the supporters of Free Enterprise, Marxist against anti-Marxist. The same divisions may be traced to periods more remote and regions of historical study with even less apparent connection with modern quarrels.

This element in modern historical writing is neither particularly reprehensible nor particularly dangerous. In one form or another it has nearly always been there. In his inaugural lecture at Aberdeen Professor Sayles showed how completely a particular set of mid-nineteenth-century political and religious convictions governed the approach of Bishop Stubbs to the middle ages in spite of his vast learning, his Germanic respect for science, and his often praised dispassionateness. On certain subjects his mind was so completely made up that no evidence could shake him. Indeed from the eighteenth century to the present day, historians have continually marvelled at the total inability of their learned colleagues to see what they do not wish to see. The thing is neither so reprehensible nor so ridiculous as so bald a statement may make it seem. The finest historians are those whose imaginative insight best enables them to relate the various aspects of their knowledge and to argue from these results. They are almost inevitably very strongly bound to the ideas which they have evolved, and it is generally speaking true, that the most interesting thinkers among historians find it difficult, if not impossible, to remain open-minded about the results of their thought. Historical writing is indeed most vigorous at those epochs when modern opinions are most strongly divided. There is undoubtedly a connection between the strength and comprehensiveness of modern political, economic and even religious disputes and the vigorous flourishing of historical literature and historical scholarship in England at the present time.

I do not believe the tendency to be dangerous because I believe it to be an inseparable part of historical thinking, and least harmful when it is most obvious. The concealed prejudice is far more dangerous than the evident one. I do not think it is reprehensible because it has often been a source both of vigorous thought and vigorous writing in the past and is clearly having the same effect today. There is of course a clear distinction to be made between two very different approaches. There is the historian who sincerely seeks out the truth, although within the framework of his own ideas and beliefs. (After all, we have to have a framework of ideas and beliefs; we cannot work in any other way.) There is the political propagandist who is deliberately looking only for such facts as will support his own modern thesis. On the surface it would appear that the distinction could very easily be drawn. In fact the frontier is vague and shifting, and it is too easy to fall into the pleasant error of assuming that only one's opponents cook the evidence. By and large, and within the limits set by human fallibility, historians of all kinds and views are honest men, though capable of a good deal of self deception.

Probably the most controversial figure at the present

moment is Mr. A. L. Rowse, because he stands very much in the centre of the ancient argument about popular history, and the current political quarrels. A scholar of deep and comprehensive knowledge, a writer of unusual and various talents, he is also the holder of vigorous modern opinions. He sees no objection to introducing into his work phrases of modern colloquial use whenever he thinks they will add to the vividness of his presentation. In the same way he will flash in a parenthesis on modern politics in the midst of describing the Elizabethan scene. Violently and sometimes bitterly criticised, as vehemently praised and defended, he rides the stormy seas of his own great popularity. Of that there is no question. He has the ear of the public, and though he sometimes bellows into the public ear and sometimes tweaks it in exasperation, the public, aware of what is good for them and taking it all in good part, continue to read him. He is one of the few historians writing today who fulfils one allowable and indeed important function of the historian: he exhorts, he draws comparisons, he never lets the reader forget that he is the inheritor of all this history, that it belongs to him and he to it, that he is still in it, up to the neck.

Oddly enough for a writer who revels in the sharpness and spontaneousness, the very looseness of colloquial English, he is also, where the mood of the passage calls for it, the most meditative and lyrical of writers; sometimes poet, sometimes controversialist, he has something of the wholly personal, fierce insight of Carlyle and he seems to have found in the manysidedness, the subtlety and passion of the Elizabethan age a subject that suits his temperament and on which for that very reason, he is able to throw a brilliant, shifting light.

Style and manner are very often closely connected to the quality and character of the historian's thought. Forty years ago, in those delightful lectures which were later re-printed as *The Art of Writing*, Sir Arthur Quiller-Couch showed in a famous passage how the ambiguities and abstractions of the late Professor Freeman's writing, on certain subjects at least, reflected very clearly the ambiguities of his thought and the unreality of his deductions.

This connection between clear thought and good style is well illustrated today in Sir Lewis Namier's spare and graceful style, which reflects the analytical clean-edged quality of his thought. Never a word too many, never an irrelevant idea. He may justly claim to have exercised the greatest influence of any living historian on certain technical aspects of research. He has even given a word to the language. To 'namierise' an epoch is to enquire deeply and thoroughly into the biographical detail behind it, to break down movements, groups, political parties into the individuals who composed them, and by classifying and re-examining the details to recreate a new picture of the whole based on a detailed understanding of the parts. This technique he first displayed with mastery in *The Structure of Politics at the Accession of George III*, a book which for the last generation has had deep and widespread influence on historical enquiry far outside the eighteenth century and outside the circle of Namier's own pupils and disciples. For English history and for Parliamentary history in particular, it has been one of the great events of our time. Since the war Sir Lewis has been engaged on the great History of Parliament, but he gives us from time to time essays and reviews in which the full range of his analytical and critical powers and of a knowledge and experience which extends from the eighteenth century to modern European politics is superbly displayed. He has also published since the war a valuable monograph on Germany in 1848, a work in which once again his minute attention to the small details which make up the whole picture give a new perspective to a subject which had lent itself far too easily to Liberal or anti-liberal generalization.

When Carlyle described history as the quintessence of biographies he had nothing like 'namierisation' in mind. But one of the most interesting developments of recent years has been the reintegration of serious biographical research into the business of scientific history. The tendency up to the war, which still persists in some quarters, was to turn away from the study of individuals towards the study of political movements, social trends, economic situations, built up as far as possible from the dispassionate evidence (if it is dispassionate) of graphs and statistics.

It would seem now that the human element is coming back into history in a more businesslike and less fanciful manner. The enquiring historian begins to probe into the small and multitudinous human lives which lie behind such things as changes in methods of agriculture, the rising value of land, the rise of an urban middle class or the decline of the feudal aristocracy. The progressive de-personalization of history is at the moment held in check by this counter development.

It would be very unjust to imply that the movement towards the impersonal approach in history was mistaken or fruitless. It has cleared the ground of much romantic and valueless speculation, and induced a much cooler and more businesslike approach to what will probably long remain the most controversial as well as the most popular field of historical study, the social and economic.

In social and economic history the last years have probably seen the greatest advances. It is nearly fifteen years since G. M. Trevelyan fitly crowned a lifetime's work by his *Social History of England*, a work conceived and executed with so absolute a certainty of intention and style as to make it at once a classic. On the economic side the first volume of Sir John Clapham's *Economic History of England* (published posthumously) gathered together and gave to the general public, as well as the history student, a comprehensive picture of an essential aspect of history of which they had hitherto been but spasmodically aware. After his death, the second volume was added by Professor Court.

This enormously whetted the appetite of the public for more and more information of the kind. For many, a new dimension had been added to history. There had of course been social and economic history at an earlier time. There was always Macaulay's justly famous chapter on England in 1680. But social and even economic history were more often than not added as a kind of additional garnish to political history without being properly integrated into it. Trevelyan's *Social History* marked the final triumph rather than the beginnings of the attempt to broaden the scope of history. It made the public aware of how much was known, how much could be discovered in the daily life of his ancestors, and how much was deeply interesting. Miss Gladys Scott-Thomson, in the thirties, was a pioneer in introducing to the public the delights of social history to be found in the rich archives of a great family. Her work in the Woburn archives started a new kind of documented social history which has been much imitated.

For the last years 'comprehensiveness' of approach has been the aim of all historians writing for the general public. The social and economic pictures are organically connected with the political story; few to-day would set out in a general history to write merely a political account.

The strength of English historical writing lies in narrative, description and practical exposition. It is at its best when dealing with facts, at its weakest on theories and ideas. This partly explains the coolness with which Arnold Toynbee's completed work has been received by those professional historians who reviewed it, a coolness which was not reflected in the acceptance accorded it by the general public. The *Study of History* belongs truly rather to the realm of ideas than to history as generally understood and practised in England. Any work of this magnitude is bound to be open to criticism on points of detail. The *Study of History* is ultimately not a work of strict historical analysis, but the attempt of one man of vast scholarship, retentive memory and a philosophic habit of mind, to subjugate his entire knowledge of the past to a comprehensible pattern. In doing this Professor Toynbee has impressed upon the gigantic panorama of history certain contemporary anxieties. He has not been able to to escape from a point of view and a type of interpretation which is essentially his own. The pattern arises not from history itself but from his organization and interpretation of historical facts. It is a personal philosophy in terms of history. It is a nobly conceived attempt to make history answer the unanswerable questions about the meaning of life itself and the purpose of man's existence on this planet.

Such a task is far outside the more modest limit which even the greatest of English historians have been accustomed to set themselves. Philosophy of history has never been popular and never been very well understood in England, and it is to this kind of history that Toynbee's great work belongs.

It is impossible to conceive of world history at all without some kind of dominating idea or controlling pattern. In the nature of things this idea or pattern is more likely to be in the mind of the historian from the first than to arise spontaneously from the vast and sprawling evidences of the past. For this reason the criticism directed at Professor Toynbee's handling of facts seems largely irrelevant. What he has given us is not strictly speaking a Study of History but thoughts arising out of the study of history. What I believe that later generations will derive from his work is a certain inspiration and strength in living which we—and they—may very badly need. This is quite as important in its own right as the mere scrupulous notation of facts, with all the exceptions as well as all the rules.

The late R. C. Collingwood, influenced by Croce whose principal disciple he was in this country, and in revolt against the Cambridge school of modern philosophy, taught that modern philosophy would have to be founded on historical thinking. But with Collingwood, as with Croce, the history that he wrote himself gives very little enlightenment as to how he meant the historian to perform his new task as priest-philosopher of mankind. His early book on Roman Britain and the curious fragment on the Albigenses in his *New Leviathan* (his last important work written when he was already a sick man) give little idea of the luminous depth of knowledge which those who heard him lecture at Oxford between the wars will not forget.

The early death of Collingwood left us without a philosopher historian of the first rank. In the last ten years the gap has been partly filled by Professor Butterfield. There have been other influences of course. The belated translation of Burckhardt's *Lectures on History* has at last put the subtle, ranging, exploratory ideas of one of the greatest of nineteenth-century thinkers within reach of the English history student. The translation of Marc Bloch's last work—those thoughts on history written at odd hours during the dangers and sufferings of the Resistance—has made the younger generation not only attentive to his ideas about history in general, but may have encouraged them to learn more about his influence and his achievement in mediaeval studies in France.

But the cautious and conscientious voice of Professor Butterfield, although it is never raised very loud, is becoming the one to which more thoughtful historians are turning to listen. His technique is to enquire into the historiography of the past and to examine, with infinite patience, the mistakes that have been made and the reasons for which they were made. He is a very quiet thinker and he does not cultivate arresting turns of style or a provocative way of thinking. One feels that he would willingly offend no man, and the driving force behind his thought sometimes seems to be a Puritan conscience. But he has shown very clearly that the striving towards an ideal of dispassionateness cannot simply be given up on the grounds that it is impossible of achievement; it is none the less something to be aimed at, for without it there is no hope of knowing the whole truth. He has gently drawn attention to the shortcomings of the best historical methods and the highest techniques until our habits of thought are more honest and conscious. We believe ourselves to be open-minded without being so. With all the advantages of modern research, we are still only too ready to ram new evidence into the old pattern which suits us, without seeing that any new evidence calls for a reconsideration of *all* the evidence; the relationship between all the pieces must be modified by the addition of a new one. Furthermore he asserts with ever greater conviction that the ultimate aim of history is towards world history and world comprehension. Fragmentary and specialized knowledge is of ultimate value only in relation to a greater whole.

The works of Professor Butterfield—*Christianity and History* and *Man on his Past*—are in some ways out of key with the note of provocative certainty which is most common in history today. Strong in our techniques of research, sustained by card indexes, assisted by microfilms, resting our conclusions on an ever increasing bulk of sifted, calendared, registered documents, we historians grow very pleased with ourselves. Some of us are further sustained by the pleasures of literary success and the evident interest of the public, others by the support and approval of colleagues and pupils. All this has led to great vigour and assurance in modern historical writing, has created an energy which spills over into fruitful and violent arguments between schools of thought. We stand in need of honest painful thought (using painful in its seventeenth-century sense), of doubt and humility, and perhaps also of fewer political ideas and stronger moral ideals.

The Literature of
Ideas

—

MAURICE CRANSTON

T HE KEY NAME to the recent history of British
philosophy is a foreign one: that of Ludwig Wittgenstein. A rich, eccentric Austrian Jew, Wittgenstein first came to England in 1909 to study engineering at Manchester; there he developed an interest in logic
and went on to Cambridge, where Bertrand Russell was
writing his *Principia Mathematica* and G. E. Moore
was working out his 'commonsense' philosophy by the
socratic technique of free discussion.[1] Wittgenstein
learned all these men had to teach, went back to the continent, served in the Austrian Army in the 1914 war, and
then 'retired' from philosophy. However, after some
persuasion from Russell, he allowed his book *Tractatus
Logico-Philosophicus* to be published in London in 1922,
and later he gave interviews to some Austrian admirers
of the book who had formed the so-called Vienna Circle.
In 1929 Wittgenstein returned to Cambridge, where he
was elected one of the two Professors of Philosophy. He

---

[1] The most useful introduction to the work of Russell and Moore
is provided by *The Philosophy of Bertrand Russell* and *The Philosophy of G. E. Moore,* omnibus volumes both edited by Paul
Schillp.

gave instruction only to a few hand-picked pupils and published nothing other than one unimportant article. In the second war he became a hospital orderly (having already given away his fortune on Tolstoian principles) and after the war he resigned from his university chair. He died in 1950.

Wittgenstein's *Tractatus*, a bewildering oracular work, did not bring about an immediate change in the British approach to philosophy. A greater stir was caused in 1936 by A. J. Ayer's *Language, Truth and Logic*. This luminously intelligible book by an Oxford don of 26 introduced the English-reading public to the doctrine which the Vienna Circle had developed out of the *Tractatus*: logical positivism. Although logical positivism was thus of immediate foreign origin, it belonged to an essentially British tradition. The line can be traced right back through Russell, Mill, Hume, Berkeley and Locke to Bacon. Empiricism of one kind or another was dominant in English philosophy until the coming of Hegelian Idealism in the nineteenth century, and outside academic circles empiricism has always been characteristic of the English mind (if one may speak of so unempirical an entity) in contrast to the continental mind. Logical positivism is empiricism pushed to extremes. The empiricist looks to science for knowledge; the logical positivist says that anything which is not science is nonsense. Ayer declared roundly in *Language, Truth and Logic* that the judgements of ethics and aesthetics are no more than expressions of emotion, which can be neither true nor false; that any statement about God is literally meaningless; and that the traditional problems of philosophy are pseudo-problems.

But when Ayer's book appeared in 1936 Wittgenstein's

own ideas were no longer, if they had ever been, the same as those of the Vienna Circle. His *Tractatus* contained the seeds of something other and more constructive than logical positivism. In place of the old notion of a philosophy as a system, Wittgenstein was developing at Cambridge the idea of 'philosophy as an activity', as a technique of clarifying understanding by investigating the internal logic of statements. This new way of doing philosophy has come to be known as 'analysis'. Its emergence owes much to the influence of G. E. Moore on Wittgenstein. Wittgenstein took his mathematics and formal logic from Russell; but Moore, who is neither a scientist nor a mathematician, taught him his 'informal logic,' and Wittgenstein was following a lead given by Moore when he directed the philosopher's attention to the close study of the ordinary use of language, to common speech. Wittgenstein still agreed with the logical positivists that there is no point in talking in general terms about, for example, the problem of immortality, but he did think there was much to be gained by discussing such questions as: 'What do we mean when we say that somebody survives?'

The history of English philosophy in the past twenty years has been one of the swift rise of logical positivism followed by its progressive modification in favour of analysis. Logical positivism flourished in Vienna as a reaction against the extreme Germanic cult of metaphysics, especially Hegelian Idealism. In England there was no such great power to overthrow. The spokesmen of metaphysics in England between the wars were the hesitant and equivocal champions of such doctrines as realism (dominant at Oxford), pragmatism, vitalism. F. H. Bradley, the greatest of English Idealists, had died

in 1924, his immediate influence spent. R. C. Collingwood, though closer to Croce than to Bradley, upheld the
Hegelian tradition in Oxford until his death in 1943, but,
as the head of his college said, there had been 'a great
gulf' between Collingwood and his 'philosophical colleagues'.

Ironically perhaps, the Hegelianism of Bradley and
Collingwood has stood up to the onslaughts of positivism
and the tests of analysis better than the once fashionable
realism; and such books as Bradley's *Appearance and
Reality* and *Ethical Studies* and Collingwood's *Philosophical Method*, *Principles of Art* and *The New Leviathan* are gaining yearly in prestige. Apart from H. H.
Price's seminal *Perception*, most of the works of Collingwood's 'philosophical colleagues' at Oxford are already
forgotten.

Analysis, unlike logical positivism, does not dismiss all
metaphysical statements as nonsense or all ethical statements as meaningless. Even the principal importer and
exponent of logical positivism, A. J. Ayer himself, has
changed his original attitude considerably. He has abandoned his old dogmatism and is now much more moder-
ate than many other analysts. His collected *Philosophical
Essays* published in 1954, was officially described as being
concerned with 'questions in logic and metaphysics'.

Three of the most important books which have come
out of the analytical school are about ethics: *Ethics and
Language* by C. L. Stevenson, *The Language of Morals*
by R. M. Hare, and *Ethics* by Patrick Nowell-Smith.
Nevertheless, there is a great difference between 'ethics'
as these writers understand the word and ethics as many
philosophers of the past have understood it; for analytic
philosophers ethics is not the science of conduct but the

study of the language of moral judgements; 'ethics' has become meta-ethics.

It is difficult for many people to understand why modern English philosophers spend their time discussing words; it is indeed impossible to see the value of the method unless it is seen in action. Gilbert Ryle's *The Concept of Mind* would probably give a better idea of what it is all about than any systematic exposition; although J. O. Urmson's *Philosophical Analysis: Its Development Between the Two World Wars* is an excellent historical study, the only up-to-date exposition available is *The Revolution in Philosophy* edited by D. F. Pears.[1] Wittgenstein's own posthumous book *Philosophical Investigations* is a disappointing one, and the philosophy student at an English university has to rely largely on articles in the learned journals: *Mind, Analysis, Philosophy*, and *The Proceedings of the Aristotelian Society*.

The influence of Wittgenstein has had its good side and its bad side. It has cleared out the waffling and bogus elements, and introduced new discipline, vigour and austerity into British philosophy. It has led to great progress in symbolic logic[2] and a new liaison between philosophy and science. To give but one example, J. Z. Young's book *Doubt and Certainty in Science* shows the value of philosophical analysis to a professional naturalist. Philosophy in England has ceased to be a substitute for religion.

On the other hand, a certain intolerance and narrowness, characteristic of logical positivism, is still discernible

[1] This is an entirely favourable exposition. For a hostile critique see: *The Philosophical Predicament* by W. H. F. Barnes.

[2] See, in this connection, F. Waismann's *Introduction to Mathematical Thinking*, W. Kneale's *Probability and Induction*, and P. F. Strawson's *Introduction to Logical Theory*.

in the analytic movement. There is a marked tendency, particularly in some universities, towards 'party-line' thinking, coupled with a tendency to regard any philosopher who expresses views on direct ethical (as distinct from meta-ethical) questions as an old-fashioned fuddy-duddy or a quack. What is in some ways even worse is the philistinism which has grown up with the analytic movement. Urged by Wittgenstein to study the usage of common speech, certain philosophers have conscientiously adopted the linguistic habits of the vulgar. The following paragraph from John Wisdom's *Other Minds* is by no means unrepresentative:

> How do we know when a man's angry? Not like we know a kettle's boiling—by deduction from the physical symptoms For in knowing another man's angry we use the analogy of our own feelings. But this is not to use analogy like we do when we know they're having a party opposite; for then we may ourselves be wrong; that is, to such knowledge is opposed a non-analogical, direct, knowledge.
> "Do we know a man's angry like we know the weight of thistledown? Here the weight isn't known merely from the symptoms on the scales, but from this in conjunction with having felt the weight of other things we have weighed. . .

Some readers may confront the 'mateyness' of this passage without embarrassment; but it is hard to see any justification for the excessively colloquial contraction of 'is' to ' 's' (properly confined in written language to the genitive) or the perverse misuse no less than three times in succession of the word 'like' in a way which, Fowler noted, 'every illiterate person uses daily' and which, indeed, one might have imagined only illiterate persons ever used. Ryle has made an art of the colloquial style, he is a true master of language. Others, with their 'homely' images of door-knobs, motor-cars and band-stands, their deliberate shunning of classical or literary allusions, their stern repression of anything so frivolous as wit or ornament, might almost be as many Wyke-hamist Communists trying to curry favour with an audience of proletarian dissenters.

How far—how lamentably far—is this from Collingwood's belief that philosophy is a branch of literature! Like Wittgenstein, Collingwood believed that 'the needs of philosophy can only be met by ordinary language'. But by 'ordinary language' Collingwood meant the language of civilized, discriminating men, 'a literary language', as he put it, 'and not a technical'. And yet there is no necessary connection between Collingwood's kind of philosophy and excellence of writing. Neither need there by any association of vulgarity with Wittgenstein's kind of philosophy. I have mentioned Ryle. I could also mention Bertrand Russell, a most civilized stylist. Indeed, for that matter, the original German text of the *Tractatus Logico-Philosophicus* is in its own odd way, a literary masterpiece.

The philosophers who do write well are almost always those whose interests are not limited to philosophy; the pleasing writers among post-war British philosophers are those, such as Stuart Hampshire, Richard Wollheim, Anthony Quinton and A. G. N. Flew, who have published articles on literary, historical or topical questions; or such as Patrick Gardiner and Geoffrey Warnock, who are also poets.[1] But the links between analysis and literature

[1] Good writing is also to be found in critical studies of the great philosophers: Stuart Hampshire's *Spinoza*, R. S. Peters' *Hobbes*, Karl Britton's *Mill*, Iris Murdoch's *Sartre*, Geoffrey Warnock's *Berkeley*, W. B. Gallie's *Peirce*, F. C. Coplestone's *Aquinas*.

as such are few. Two distinguished philosophers of the analytic school, Isaiah Berlin and John Holloway, have, in *The Hedgehog and the Fox* and *The Victorian Sage* respectively, made important contributions to literary criticism, but either might conceivably have written as he did without a specific training in philosophy. Possibly, again, some crumbs from Wittgenstein's table may have nourished the 'scientific' school of literary criticism, according to which it is possible to be a critic without having any taste; and the more aggressively philistine of the young provincial novelists are reported to have been 'influenced by logical positivism', but in neither case is there evidence of an important connection, unless the curious desire of the heroes of the provincial novels to become, like Wittgenstein, male hospital orderlies is a sign of anything significant.

Wittgenstein can, however, be seen as an extreme case of something which has been wholly characteristic of English intellectual life in recent years. That is the trend away from comprehensive system-building towards piecemeal study of detail. It is true that Arnold Toynbee has lately completed his all-embracing *Study of History*, but although his learning is universally admired, Toynbee's book has been sharply criticized, not only from the point of view of philosophical analysis by Patrick Gardiner (in *The Nature of Historical Explanation*) but also by a large number of historians themselves. It is also true that Fred Hoyle, in *The Nature of the Universe*, has put forward, with the approval of several other Cambridge physicists, a new cosmology; but Hoyle has learned from the example of Eddington and Jeans (who were unhorsed as metaphysicians by Susan Stebbing in *Philosophy and the Physicists*), not to claim too much authority for his speculations.

Nowhere has the trend towards specialization been more marked than in the field of economics. Between the wars the books of J. M. Keynes and his contemporaries not only dealt with fairly general principles but were intelligible to the lay public. A typical book by an economist today is largely composed of symbols and curves, and is so esoteric that no one except an economics graduate with minute knowledge of the author's own fragment of the field can possibly understand it. One or two British economists, however, have refused to be circumscribed by the new limitations of their subject and have produced books of the old synoptic and intelligible kind. *The Theory of Economic Growth* by W. Arthur Lewis, *Britain's Economic Problems* by C. A. R. Crosland and *The Common Sense of Political Economy* by Lionel Robbins are the outstanding examples. R. F. Harrod's *Keynes* might also be mentioned in connection with these matters.

What is true of economics is only a little less true of psychology. The narrowing of the theory has been accompanied by a diminution of the stature of the theorists. The days of great creative thinkers like MacDougall and William James seem to be over. The best things that have appeared in English psychological literature in the past twenty years have been conscientious studies of specific problems—such books as G. E. Humphrey's *Thinking*, W. Tinbergen's *Study of Instinct*, M. D. Vernon's *Visual Perception*, and Kenneth Craik's *The Nature of Explanation*. Again, as in philosophy, historical studies have been among the most rewarding. They include R. S. Peters' edition of G. H. Brett's *History of Psychology*, Oliver Zangwill's *Introduction to Psychology*, W. R. D. Fairbarn's *Psycho-analytical Studies of the Personality*, and Frieda Fordham's *Introduction to Jung's Psychology*.

In the field of political science and sociology the movement from the comprehensive to the piecemeal has coincided with a retreat from the Left-wing ideas of Planning which were dominant until about 1945. The leading political theorists of pre-1945 period in England—Harold Laski, G. D. H. Cole, E. F. M. Durbin, E. H. Carr, Leonard Woolf—were all socialists of one sort or another. The influence of Shaw and Wells was still great, and up to 1939 at any rate there was a considerable public for such out-and-out Marxist books as *The Theory and Practice of Socialism* by John Strachey and *Illusion and Reality* by Christopher Caudwell. The appearance in 1945 of Karl Popper's *The Open Society and its Enemies*, signalized a new departure. A man of Austrian birth, Popper had been influenced in his younger days by Wittgenstein,[1] and his book embodied at the same time a protest against false metaphysics in philosophy with an assertion of liberal individualism against *étatisme* in politics.

Other important critiques of Marxism and Marxist historicism have been published by English scholars in the past few years. They include Popper's own *The Poverty of Historicism*, Isaiah Berlin's *Historical Inevitability*, and H. B. Acton's *The Illusion of the Epoch*. On the other hand, the best critical accounts of the practice as distinct from the theory of Communism are to be found in more popular books, notably in those by Arthur

---

[1] Popper's mature philosophical views are, however, sharply at variance with those of Wittgenstein and the philosophical analysts. In the absence of adequate bound literature on this subject the reader must be referred to the quarterly periodical *The British Journal of the Philosophy of Science*. J. O. Wisdom's *Foundations of Inference in Natural Science* owes much to Popper's teaching as does the work of J. W. N. Watkins.

Koestler (chiefly, but not only *The Yogi and the Commissar*) and by George Orwell.

An attempt to bring together the threads of analytical philosophy and political liberalism was made by the short-lived quarterly magazine *Polemic*, but the only *general* book on political theory by a new-model philosophy don as yet is *The Vocabulary of Politics* by T. D. Weldon, who refuses to take sides on the issue of liberalism *versus* totalitarianism. Weldon argues that 'most of the questions of traditional political philosophy are . . . confused formulations of purely empirical difficulties' and further that 'writers on political institutions and statesmen, not philosophers, are the proper people to deal with them'. This desire to cut the moralist out of politics altogether seems to me to establish Weldon as a logical positivist rather than an analytical philosopher. Analysis is neither anti-moral nor anti-rational—a point which is made by Stephen Toulmin in *The Place of Reason in Ethics* and in the special symposium on 'Reason' published in *The Political Quarterly* for Summer 1955.

The London School of Economics, once the home of the Left-wing Planners, has since the war become a stronghold of their opponents. Among important anti-Left books by its teachers are F. A. Hayek's *The Road to Serfdom* and J. L. Talmon's *The Origins of Totalitarian Democracy*. Popper has been Professor of Logic at the London School of Economics since 1949, and in 1951 Michael Oakeshott succeeded Harold Laski as Professor of Political Science. Oakeshott is not only against the Left; he is a positive champion of the Right. Like Coleridge, Oakeshott is an Idealist in metaphysics as well as a conservative in politics. His success represents not only a reaction against socialism, but also a return (in an unlikely place) to the tradition of Bradley and Colling-wood. His introduction to the Blackwell reprint of Hobbes's *Leviathan* and his pamphlet *Political Education* are his only political writings in bound form, but the files of the *Cambridge Journal*, which Oakeshott edited from 1948 until its extinction in 1953, afford some insight into the workings of his mind; he is a brilliant literary journalist.

Another theorist of the Right, not less distinguished than Michael Oakeshott, is Herbert Butterfield, Master of Peterhouse, Cambridge. In a series of books, including *The Statecraft of Machiavelli*, *Christianity and History*, and *Christianity, Diplomacy and War*, Butterfield has presented an original, and in many ways a startling synthesis of Machiavellian realism and Christian pessimism. Such books as A. L. Rowse's *The End of an Epoch*, T. S. Eliot's *The Idea of a Christian Society* and L. S. Amery's *Thoughts on the Constitution* represent other, and perhaps more widely acceptable forms of conservative opinion.

In religious thought the trend has been away from the modernism and latitudinarianism of such men as Charles Raven and the younger William Temple towards strict and orthodox theology. When Bishop Barnes's *The Rise of Christianity* appeared in 1947, its reception showed that his kind of liberal, sceptical Christianity was already outmoded. Existentialism, which has had no influence whatever on British philosophy, has strengthened a reaction of Nonconformist Protestant theology against rationalism and in the direction of more rigid fideism. C. S. Lewis's immensely popular *Screwtape Letters*, his more specialized book on *Miracles*, T. S. Eliot's *Thoughts after Lambeth* and other essays on religious subjects, and

Basil Willey's *Christianity Past and Present* are all written from the High Church or Anglo-Catholic standpoint. At the same time there has been a marked quickening of public interest in the work of Roman Catholic writers such as Ronald Knox, Martin D'Arcy, Bede Griffiths, Thomas Gilbey, David Kelly and Frederick Coplestone.

This movement of religious opinion towards more dogmatic forms of belief cannot be explained in terms of the period in which it has happened. It is part of something which dates back to the nineteenth century—an epoch of moral certainty but also an epoch of religious questioning and doubt. The 'Sea of Faith' which was 'out' when Matthew Arnold wrote *Dover Beach* a hundred years ago went farther out in later decades, and was farthest out in the 1920's; then, when moral certainty as well as religious certainty had ebbed to an extent which seemed to many people dangerous, the 'Sea of Faith' began—not everywhere, but in places, and interesting places—to turn.

The Progress of
Translation

ERIK DE MAUNY

IN ALMOST EVERY age, translation has figured as a
poor relation of literature, its practitioners labouring
in the shadows, and only the most tireless and devoted
succeeding finally in catching a pale reflection of their
original's glory. Nor, since Tytler wrote his excellent
Essay on the Principles of Translation in the late eighteenth century, to lament and in some measure repair
this neglect, have many others troubled to review the
problem as a whole. It is perfectly understandable. By its
very nature, translation should be a transparency; the
better it is done, the less it attracts the reader's notice;
so that, to talk about translation at all is rather like talking about the glass in front of a picture, when it is the
picture itself that engrosses our attention.

Thus the elusiveness of the subject presents an initial
difficulty: it seems to me that translation can only be
discussed in relation to a whole complex of other factors,
which together make up the climate of a period. Nevertheless, once this difficulty has been admitted, I think it
is still possible to advance one or two general propositions.
One is that every age gets the translations it deserves.

The second is that the remarkable progress that has taken place in this little-acclaimed art over the past thirty years entitles us to look upon this as one of the great ages in English translation. Naturally, such a claim begs a number of questions, particularly in view of that fond bias by which each generation imagines itself endowed with a response to life more sensitive and immediate than that of its predecessors. Furthermore, between six and seven hundred new translations now appear in this country every year: clearly only a handful reach the highest standards. In the space of a single chapter, one can do no more than indicate a few of the more notable achievements.

For, if the field has become a crowded one, there are still a certain few who tower head and shoulders above the rest, of whom Constance Garnett and C. K. Scott Moncrieff are perhaps the most eminent. Yet eminence is not really the right word, for, as I have suggested, the finer the translator, the more successfully he effaces himself. A better way of conveying the scope of their achievement might be to say that it consists in this: that we no longer consider it extraordinary that two such profoundly un-English temperaments as those of Dostoevsky and Proust should be so thoroughly acclimatized in this country. (In the case of Constance Garnett, one is even obliged to go further, and to point out that, but for her single-handed efforts, a whole generation or more of English readers might never have stumbled upon the huge, enthralling, unsuspected landscape of the Russian novel.)

In this light, one begins to see the perpetual invitation and challenge of translation. It would be wrong, of course, to underestimate its toll in hours of unrewarding drudgery; and I suspect that most translators must at some time have shared the weariness and distaste that Edwin Muir speaks of in his autobiography: 'We turned ourselves into a sort of translation factory. . . . It began as a resource and hardened into a necessity'. Nor is it surprising that the most devoted translator should come to have a somewhat equivocal and even irritable attitude towards the recreated figures on whom he has lavished such pains. Unfortunately, few translators have left any detailed record of their midnight struggles. On this score, none was more reticent than Scott Moncrieff, but the German writer E. R. Curtius has given a sufficiently vivid picture of meeting him in Rome:

> The Via della Croce—which cuts through old papal Rome from the Piazza di Spagna to the Corso—was for him a complete universe in which all human wants could be satisfied. In this animated narrow street he occupied two somewhat gloomy and dusty rooms, their outward appearance suggesting that the inmate had settled in Rome for ever and a day. By the dim light of a little lamp, and the smell—so characteristic of Rome in winter—of a reluctantly burning oil stove, he sat at a table buried under books and papers, leaving just enough room for a half-emptied *fiasco* of Chianti. He generally received me with some strong abuse of Albertine, whose moods and vicious habits were at that time keeping him very busy: he was translating one of the last volumes of Proust. The world of Proust was to him as familiar as the Via della Croce, and he roamed in it with the same enjoyment, though with a sarcastic want of respect. For though he esteemed the artist to whom he had given years of his life and the most arduous labour, he allowed little of that to be felt. A dominating, brilliantly humorous mood was his usual attitude, whether it was a question of Proust, the latest newspaper rumours, or social events. . . .

Perhaps more than in any other form of literary activity, translation is rather like travelling across a plain: for much of the way the going is tedious enough, but every now and then one comes upon a ravine where a secret river flashes out of concealment, or sees against the horizon an unknown mountain range glowing with unearthly fires. One understands then its attraction for some of the subtlest and most original minds of our time. The years that Proust spent on his translations from Ruskin, for example, were to furnish him with many rich strands of speculation for *A la Recherche du Temps Perdu*; and here is Gide noting in his *Journal* (27 July 1942): 'I am devoting the best part of my time to the translation of *Hamlet*. This is the only work in which I am able to find some distraction from my cares'; and in a later entry (1st September 1942): 'Finished yesterday the translation of *Hamlet*. Twenty years have passed since I translated the first act . . . which alone gave me more trouble than the five acts of *Anthony and Cleopatra*. . . .' Similarly, in recent years, poets like Louis MacNeice, Stephen Spender, C. Day Lewis, Rex Warner and Roy Campbell have all produced notable new translations from the classics or from contemporary literature.

Nevertheless, it is perhaps deceptive merely to talk of individual translators, without considering those gradual changes in the climate of opinion which have produced an audience for their work: and here, one must revert to the proposition that every generation gets the translations it deserves. In the social context, the most significant change has undoubtedly been the abandonment of that attitude of comfortable superiority from which the English for so many generations surveyed their European neighbours. It is true that during the whole of the classical 'Grand Tour' period, there existed a small highly-cultivated élite who spoke and used French or German as natural means of civilized intercourse. Yet we are all familiar with that other figure, the 'unhappy traveller' who, in a memorable essay by V. S. Pritchett, 'is travelling not for pleasure but for pain, not to broaden the mind but, if possible, to narrow it; to release the buried terrors and hatreds of a lifetime; or, if these have already had a good airing at home, to open up colonies of rage abroad'. Fortunately, such a figure is no longer typical; we have, in fact, recognized ourselves as common sufferers in the fate of being Europeans. The English, in short, while continuing to pride themselves on a staunch insularity, are today perhaps the least insular of peoples, and having once pushed out in a great flood over the world, are now experiencing a returning flood as vast and incalculable in its final implications.

But while all this has been happening, another transformation, less easily detected yet no less radical, has been taking place in our attitude to language itself. To trace all the contributory causes of that change would demand a separate and very much longer study: so it must suffice here simply to point to the secret relationship that exists between phenomena occurring in apparently distinct fields. I mean, for example, that movement in philosophy which has led to the replacement of the absolute by the relative; in painting and music, the advent of impressionism and all that has followed in the atomization of vision and sound; and in literature, the efforts of Joyce, Proust and Virginia Woolf to render the flow of consciousness and the intermittences and exaltations of the instinctual life.

Meanwhile, in the narrower field of purely literary studies, scholars have probed ever deeper below the surface of language, in the attempt to reveal the innermost mechanisms of literary expression. A work like R. A. Sayce's *Style in French Prose*, for example, provides a close and sensitive analysis of the changing rhythms and patterns of French literature over five centuries, from Rabelais to Proust, and demonstrates how a single word or phrase from the pen of a particular author (*énergie* in the case of Diderot, *seul, sauvage, impénétrable* with Rousseau) may offer a vital clue to understanding the temper of an age. Martin Turnell's *The Novel in France* offers another example of that enlightened scrutiny of the text itself that was once the almost exclusive preserve of commentators of Shakespeare; and there are a number of others. Their principal virtue is to remind us that, just as the personality of an individual may be compounded of many pasts, assumed and tried for a while and then discarded, so words carry within themselves the faint reverberations of long-dead voices and the echoes of past meanings that never wholly forsake them. I am not suggesting, of course, that every translator automatically rushes to such studies for guidance. Nevertheless, they play a necessary part in preparing the ground on which good translation flourishes; so that it seems unlikely, to say the least, that anyone nowadays would fall into the error of an early translator of Madame de Sévigné, who deduced from the spelling '*Thuileries*' that Marie Antoinette must have spoken with an Irish accent!

In an ideal world, it should be possible for translator and author to meet and discuss the innumerable problems that arise whenever one endeavours to recreate an original work in a language not its own. One may even imagine a centre organized on the lines of the famous

Décades at Pontigny between the wars, where such exchanges could flourish in an atmosphere vibrant with common interests and sympathies. A few translators, it is true, have enjoyed the benefit of such close personal contact. Dorothy Bussy's translations of virtually all the major works of André Gide provide a particular instance, where long friendship lent a special insight into the interpretation of those complicated and sometimes disconcerting alternations of viewpoint that marked the progression of Gide's thought.

On the whole, such contacts have been most frequent and fruitful between this country and France, so that one tends to think of many of the major French writers of this century as closely linked with their English translators. It is through the elegantly turned translations of Gerard Hopkins that we have been made familiar with Mauriac, with that charged and sultry world where pagan noon lies forever in ambush about the lonely households of the elects of guilt. Stuart Gilbert has introduced us to the packed social canvas of Roger Martin du Gard's *Les Thibault*, and to Malraux's stark newsreel vision of the plight of political man. Eric Sutton showed masterly skill in handling the complexities of Sartre's gaunt despairing novel-cycle of the Munich era, *Les Chemins de la Liberté*. I have mentioned here the works by which these three translators are perhaps best known, although all three have further claims on the English reader's gratitude. Stuart Gilbert, for instance, is a translator of extraordinarily wide range: the plays and novels of Camus, the novels of Simenon, the autobiographical writings of Saint-Exupéry, and the dense and intricate imagery of Malraux's 'Imaginary Museum' have all been grist to his mill. Gerard Hopkins has also given us

stylish versions of some of the greatest novels of nine-
teenth- and twentieth-century French fiction, his latest
work being a finely-phrased (although in a few places
oddly erratic) translation of Proust's early novel, *Jean
Santeuil*.

These are, as it were, signposts along the main highway
of French literature. But every reader will recall individual examples of the translator's tact and skill, and I
can only mention a few that have struck me as outstanding for one reason or another. Among these I would
include Kathleen Raine's translations from Balzac, notably *Lost Illusions*; Sir Edward Marsh's *Dominique*; the
delicate translations of Rosamond Lehmann; Alan Pryce-
Jones's version of Supervielle's *The Colonel's Children*;
Jean Stewart's recent translations of André Chamson and
of that brilliant curiously un-French writer, Pierre
Gascar; and, among some of the most charming but
elusive texts that any translator has had to face, Roger
Senhouse's versions of the novels of Colette, and Julian
Maclaren Ross's assured interpretation of the highly
idiosyncratic world of Raymond Queneau.

French poetry since Baudelaire has bristled with difficulties for the translator, yet there have been several
notable ventures. Among the more successful I would
include Norman Cameron's version of *A Season in Hell*,
which shows remarkable fidelity, although inevitably
some of the delirious tumult of the original leaks away.
Roy Campbell has produced a number of strikingly good
translations from Baudelaire. But it seems to me that the
finest achievement in this field in recent years has been
C. Day Lewis's version of Valéry's *Le Cimitière Marin*,
which in repeated readings has given me so much pleasure that I cannot forebear to quote a stanza:

Ils ont fondu dans une absence épaisse,
L'argile rouge a bu la blanche espèce,
Le don de vivre a passé dans les fleurs!
Où sont des morts les phrases familières,
L'art personnel, les âmes singulières?
La larve file où se formaient des pleurs.

To an impervious nothingness they're thinned,
For the red clay has swallowed the white kind;
Into the flowers that gift of life has passed.
Where are the dead?—their homely turns of speech,
The personal grace, the soul informing each?
Grubs thread their way where tears were once composed.

In the field of Russian literature, no one has yet matched the achievement of Constance Garnett. In his autobiography, David Garnett has described how his mother's interest in Russian was aroused by a chance encounter with Russian émigrés. It is clear that she mastered the language with prodigious speed, so that the full canon of her translations finally came to cover virtually every major Russian prose writer of the nineteenth century. But if this achievement is awe inspiring, it is also faintly disquieting: how should a single translator manage to reproduce in another tongue the essence of so many different styles? There are, indeed, weaknesses in Constance Garnett's great work—stiffness of dialogue, occasionally laboured and clumsy passages—so that it is not surprising that later translators should have felt impelled to traverse afresh much of the same ground.

Among the more notable of these recent translations have been David Magarshak's versions of *Crime and Punishment*, *The Idiot*, and *The Devils* (a more accurate though perhaps less evocative rendering than *The*

Possessed for Dostoevsky's original title—*Besy*). Mr. Magarshak has also produced an admirable new version of Goncharov's *Oblomov*, in which he shows great skill in handling the subtle ramifications of Russian tenses, and in reproducing the wry humorous understatement of Goncharov's great comic novel. There have also been several new versions of Turgenev, whose limpid clarity suggests itself as a translator's delight, yet conceals subtle pitfalls for the unwary. Among those that particularly deserve mention are Gilbert Gardiner's version of *On The Eve*, Isaiah Berlin's rendering of the most poetic of Turgenev's long short stories, *First Love*, Alec Brown's version of *Rudin*, and a sensitive translation of *A Sportsman's Notebook* by Charles and Natasha Hepburn. Three other translators who have produced notably good versions from the Russian are George Reavey, Elizaveta Fen, and the Baroness Budberg.

On the whole, Russian poets have fared less well than Russian prose-writers, and for a fairly obvious reason. Maurice Baring long ago pointed out that in its simplicity and its plastic qualities, Russian poetry bears many affinities with classical Greek verse, and also mentioned its 'curious matter-of-fact quality'. But these are just the virtues that are so difficult to carry over into another tongue. Several attempts have been made to translate Pushkin into English verse. Of these, the most successful, to my thinking, is still that of Oliver Elton, whose version of *Evgeny Onegin* is, indeed, something of a triumph in that it reproduces the intricate double rhymes of the original while yet retaining its free and nonchalant movement. Some of Pushkin's shorter lyrics have also been sensitively translated by Frances Cornford and Esther Polianowsky Salaman in *Poems from the Russian*, which provides an excellent short introduction to the whole field. But of the other major Russian poets of the eighteenth and nineteenth centuries, I can think of few versions that are really outstanding—although I would make an exception for Sir Bernard Pares's delightful translations of Krylov's *Fables*.

Even among the prose-writers, there are, of course, gaps and inadequacies. It seems strange, for instance, that there is no English translation of Radishchev, in many ways a Russian counterpart of Sterne (although I believe the Soviet Foreign Languages Publishing House has recently produced one); or that a great satirist like Saltykov-Shchedrin should be known here by only one novel, *The Golovlyov Family*. Furthermore, there has been a strange neglect of writers who came to the fore in the uneasy interregnum between the 1905 and 1917 revolutions. Gorky and Chekhov have, admittedly, found several English interpreters. But how much is known of Biely, of Blok, of Sologub, whose *Little Demon* was acclaimed by Gide as one of the most fascinating novels ever to emerge from Russia? There was, indeed, an attempt to cover this ground just after the war, in Lindsay Drummond's Russian Literature series, which included translations of Blok's *The Spirit of Music*, Remizov's *On A Field Azure*, Andreyev's *The Seven Who Were Hanged*, and Pasternak's *Selected Poems*. Pasternak's collected prose works were issued by the same publisher, in translations by Beatrice Scott and Robert Payne. Herbert Marshall's copiously annotated *Mayakovsky and his Poetry* appeared at about the same time; but there is still no English edition of Essenin, who provides the essential counter-balance to Mayakovsky in the early post-revolutionary period. Of Russian émigré writers, several translations were made of Kuprin, who now seems to have been overrated; and there are sensitive versions of Bunin's *The Gentleman from San Francisco* (by S. S. Koteliansky and D. H. Lawrence), *The Well of Days* (by Gleb Struve and Hamish Miles) and other novels, which should endure. Of the Soviet period, it yet seems too early to speak, largely because of the rarity of works of real stature.

Of translations from German and Italian, I must speak more briefly, having only a very imperfect knowledge of either language. In German literature, Thomas Mann clearly stands pre-eminent, and not there alone, being in the view of many reputable critics the greatest novelist of this century. It is difficult for anyone unacquainted with the original to pass judgement on this claim. But certainly the reader gains a more than fair idea of the immense breadth and penetration of Mann's imagination in the translations of H. T. Lowe-Porter: these have always seemed to me a very solid achievement, although German-speaking friends have pointed out imperfections, and I am willing to believe that they fail to deal adequately with some of Mann's virtuoso passages in archaic and abstruse styles. In terms not only of intrinsic fascination but of their extraordinary influence on other writers, one must also give a high place to the translations from Kafka by Edwin and Willa Muir. There have been a number of fresh translations from the German classics in recent years (Philip Wayne's version of the first part of *Faust* in the Penguin Classics is a good example), and from the German poets, Heine, Hölderlin, Hofmannsthal, and Rilke. Rilke, in particular, has exercised a strong fascination over English translators, and several versions of his poems—by J. B. Leishmann, Edward and Victoria Sackville West, and others—have appeared. Of them all, those that have struck me as by far the most impressive as poems in their own right are the versions by Ruth Speirs. These have appeared in various literary journals, but unfortunately, owing to complicated copyright problems, not in book form.

In the period since the war, by far the most exciting experience provided by German literature has proved to be Eithne Wilkins' and Ernst Kaiser's translation of Robert Musil's extraordinary novel, *The Man Without Qualities*, which in its brooding examination of the problems of identity and selfhood, speaks as cogently to a world that has known the concentration camps and the annihilation of self as Kafka's novels spoke earlier to a generation straying in the blind alleys of ideology. Among other effective translations from German have been Stuart Hood's version of Ernst Jünger's *On The Marble Cliffs* and C. M. Woodhouse's translation of a powerful and sombre war novel by Herbert Zand, *The Last Sortie*. I have avoided speaking of several German novelists well-known before the war—Stefan Zweig, Anna Seghers, Ernst Wiechert—but their work is readily available in sound and readable English versions. There is, however, one other whose reputation has been rising rapidly above our horizon during the past few years: I mean Berthold Brecht. As yet, few English translations have been made from his large and immensely varied output. It will be interesting to see who takes up the challenge.

Italian literature, being relatively poor in fiction, has not traditionally offered the same scope to the translator as French, German or Russian. Nevertheless, in Dante, one may see both the supreme test of the translator's art, and a perennial source of delight that wholly oversways the numberless hours of drudgery that the task demands. In the past twenty years or so, several new versions have been made, of which the most accessible, and in many ways, the most remarkable, in its dexterity and resourcefulness within the difficult framework of *terza rima*, is that on which Dorothy Sayers is at present engaged for Penguin Books. Among other notable translations from Italian classics in recent years have been Archibald Colquhoun's new version of Manzoni's *The Betrothed*, and John Heath-Stubbs's delicate renderings of the poems of Leopardi. Two other works should be mentioned at this point: Eric Mosbacher's excellent translation of Verga's *I Malavoglia* (in English *The House by the Medlar Tree*), and the equally admirably version of Svevo's *Confessions of Zeno* by Beryl de Zoete.

Since the war, with the disappearance of fascist rule and its stultifying effect on all the arts, the Italian novel has given proof of new vigour, proof that English readers have been able to witness for themselves in translations by Bernard Wall, W. J. Strachan, Lydia Holland and others of the work of such writers as Alberto Moravia, Cesare Pavese, Vasco Pratolini and Elio Vittorini. There have also been spasmodic efforts to translate such modern Italian poets as Ungaretti, although perhaps the greatest among them, Montale, still awaits the ideal interpreter.

In this survey I have only attempted to deal, and then all too summarily, with four of the main European languages. This has the advantage of imposing a certain cohesion on a sprawling field, but many gaps obviously remain unfilled, and I must try to make token amends in a brief final space. This obligation is all the more impera-

tive in that I have not yet mentioned one of the greatest
of all achievements in translation in the present century:
Arthur Waley's versions from the Chinese. They have
had, indeed, tributes enough, so that to seek here some
brief formulary of further praise might seem almost an
impertinence. One can say only that, like a later Marco
Polo of the spirit, Arthur Waley magically found a way to
introduce his readers into that extraordinary Chinese
civilization where the scholar's or the lover's briefest
poems seem to summon forth the shades of the whole
vast empire in which they were produced.

Then, in discussing what translation has made known
to us of the literatures of France and Italy, it is scarcely
possible to pass over in silence the other main tributaries
to the Mediterranean world. In this respect—and it
matches a contemporary northern nostalgia for the clarity
and sharp definition of Mediterranean light—we have
been lucky in the past decade or two in the number and
quality of new translations from Spanish and Portuguese
and Greek. Again, there is scarcely room to deal with
them individually in detail. But among those that I feel
least able to ignore are John Mavrogordato's cleanly
chiselled translations of the Alexandrian Greek, Cavafy;
the translations of Seferis (in *The King of Asine*) by
Bernard Spencer, Lawrence Durrell and Nanos Valaoritis,
the versions of Lorca by Stephen Spender and J. L. Gili;
Gamel Wolsey's translations of Peréz Galdos; and Roy
Campbell's of Eça de Queiroz.

Finally, there are those new translations of the classics
that appear in almost every generation, clothed each
time in a new idiom, yet perpetually reasserting, as it
were, their first springtime. In this field, there has been
no more remarkable development in recent years than

the successful experiment of Penguin Books in launching a series of classics in entirely new versions. Not all of these have managed to improve to any considerable degree on earlier, but long out-of-print, versions. Yet the general standard of achievement has proved remarkably high: and in its full effect, the establishment of this series may hold a significance well beyond that of a happily inspired trial venture in book publishing. Started just after the war, under the general editorship of E. V. Rieu, the series already includes some sixty volumes, ranging from the Bible to Balzac and Flaubert. Several others in the series have already been mentioned—Dorothy Sayer's Dante and David Magarshak's translations from the Russian—and I should particularly single out Mr. Rieu's own translations of Homer and Virgil, and J. M. Cohen's excellent new versions of Rabelais and Cervantes: and all of these are available for a few shillings each. There has been nothing quite like it since Everyman's Library began, and indeed this seems to be the latest stage in the silent revolution in taste that began with that earlier and happily still flourishing series.

But one must draw a term to this account. I had not intended it to be a mere catalogue, although this was at times a danger not easily avoided; and having, perhaps, barely circumvented it, I am even then aware of having had to pass over in silence a good many admirable translations. But there, perhaps, lies the justification of my earlier claim. I do not think anyone will dispute the quality of those translations I have managed to discuss. That there should be so many worthy of note in the span of a generation or two suggests that this has indeed been one of the more remarkable ages in English translation.

Index

Namier, L., 183, 185, 198
Nature of Explanation, The, 213
Nature of Historical Explanation, The, 212
Neale, J. M., 22, 192
Nelson, 23
Neutrals, 75
New Bearings in English Poetry, 87, 146
Newby, P. H., 57
New Leviathan, 202, 208
'New Poetry', 103
New Signatures, 104
'New Soundings', 103
'New Verse', 103
New Verse, 83
New Writing, 85, 104
Nicolson, H., 21, 23–4, 36, 176, 180
Night and Day, 173
Night Fishing, The, 100
Night Mail, 99
1984, 30, 49
Nineteen Hundred and Nineteen, 108
Note in Music, A, 46
Not I, But the Wind, 17
Novel in France, The, 223
Novel on Yellow Paper, 57
Nowell-Smith, P., 208

Oakes, P., 75
Oakeshott, M., 215–16
Oblomov, 227
O'Casey, S., 31, 125, 135
Of Human Bondage, 54
Olivia, 32
Olivier, L., 129
Oman, C., 23
On a Field Azure, 228
On the Eve, 227
On the Marble Cliffs, 230

Open Society and its Enemies, The, 214
Origins of Totalitarian Democracy, The, 215
Orwell, G., 49, 156, 178, 215
Othello, 150
Other Minds, 210
Over the Bridge, 32
Owen, W., 79–80, 82, 84, 96

Palgrave, 116, 177, 179
Palmerston, 17
Paradise Lost, 155
Pares, B., 228
Pasternak, 228
Pater, W., 166, 169–70, 172–3, 177
Paulhan, J., 71
Pavesi, C., 231
Payne, R., 228
Pears, D. F., 209
Peniakov, Col., 37
Penny for a Song, 136
Perception, 208
Personal Heresy, The, 22
Personal Landscape, 111
Peters, R. S., 211, 213
Philosophical Analysis, 209
Philosophical Essays, 208
Philosophical Investigations, 209
Philosophical Method, 208
Philosophical Predicament, The, 209
Philosophy, 209
Philosophy and the Physicists, 212
Philosophy of Bertrand Russell, The, 205
Philosophy of G. E. Moore, The, 205
Picasso, 82, 96–7
Picnic at Sakhara, The, 57

Richards, I. A., 76, 99, 101, 141, 147–9, 154–6
Richardson, R., 129
Richardson, S., 62
Rickword, E., 79
Riding, L., 93
Rieu, E. V., 233
Rilke, 229
Rimbaud, 109
Rise of Christianity, The, 216
Road to Serfdom, The, 215
Road to Xanadu, The, 22
Robbins, L., 213
Robert Louis Stevenson, 22
Roger Fry, 25
Romilly, G., 38
Rose for Winter, A, 41
Ross, A., 41
Rothenstein, W., 14
Rousseau, 26, 223
Rowse, A. L., 183, 192, 197, 216
Rudin, 227
Ruins and Visions, 89
Rumour at Nightfall, 47
Runciman, S., 192
Ruskin, 20, 43, 221
Ruskin, 20
Ruskin: The Great Victorian, 20
Russell, B., 11, 205–7, 211
Rylands, S., 177
Ryle, G., 209–11

Sackville-West, E., 230
Sackville-West, V., 230
Sagan, F., 48
Saintsbury, 101
Saints Day, 136
Salaman, E. P. 227
Salinger, 60–1
Saltykov-Shchedrin, 228
Sansom, W., 54–5
Sartre, J.-P., 66, 69, 224

Sassoon, S., 29, 79, 81, 84
Savage, 16
Sayce, R. A., 223
Sayers, D., 231, 233
Sayles, Prof., 192, 195
Schillp, P., 205
Science and Poetry, 76, 154
Scott, B., 228
Scott, J. D., 57
Scott, T., 112
Scott Moncrieff, C. K., 219–20
Scott-Thomson, G., 200
Screwtape Letters, The, 216
Scrutinies, 1
Scrutiny, 146–7
Seafarer, The, 144
Season in Hell, A, 225
Seferis, 232
Seghers, A., 230
Senhouse, R., 225
Selected Poems, 228
Seventeenth Century English Literature, 177
Seven Types of Ambiguity, 149, 151
Seven Who Were Hanged, The, 228
Sévigné, Mme de, 223
Shadowy Waters, The, 81
Shakespeare, 5, 21, 27, 114, 123, 125, 128–30, 134, 136, 138, 149–50, 177, 223
Shakespeare and the Stoicism of Seneca, 155
Shaw, G. B., 48, 123, 125, 138–9, 218
Shelley, 20, 75, 116, 147, 154
Shenstone, 117
Shrimp and the Anemone, The, 51
Sidney, P., 141, 168
Sigmund Freud, 19

BELMONT COLLEGE LIBRARY

GEORGE PEABODY COLLEGE
LIBRARY
NASHVILLE, TENN.

Date Due

NOV 24 '72			
	PRINTED	IN U. S. A.	